I'm Not Toxic, You're Overreacting

A Skeptic's Guide to Recognize Harmful Behavior, Change Toxic Patterns, and Build Drama-Free Relationships Without Guilt or Self-Help Fluff

Delia Sikes

Neel Mountain Publishing

Copyright © 2025 by Delia Sikes.

All rights reserved.

No portion of this book may be reproduced in any form without written permission from the publisher or author, except as permitted by U.S. copyright law.

Legal Notice:

This book is only for personal use. No one can amend, distribute, sell, use, quote or paraphrase any part of the content within this book without the consent of the author or publisher.

Disclaimer Notice:

Under no circumstances will any blame or legal responsibility be held against the publisher, or author, for any damages, reparation, or monetary losses, direct or indirect, due to the information contained within this book, including but not limited to errors, omissions, or inaccuracies. You are responsible for your own choices, actions, and results.

Please note the information contained within this document is for educational and entertainment purposes only. All effort has been expended to present accurate, up-to-date, complete and reliable information. No warranties of any kind are declared or implied. Readers acknowledge that the author is not engaging in the rendering of legal, financial, medical or professional advice. The content within this book has been derived from various sources. Please consult a licensed professional before attempting any techniques outlined in this book.

Contents

Introduction   1

1. Recognize Toxic Behavior   4
    - 1.1 Defining Toxicity: What It Is and What It Isn't
    - 1.2 Spotting the Red Flags: Common Toxic Behaviors at Work
    - 1.3 Family Dynamics and Hidden Toxicity
    - 1.4 Bias-Driven Microaggressions: Subtle Yet Harmful
    - 1.5 Gaslighting and Its Consequences
    - 1.6 Understanding Toxic Positivity and Its Impact
    - 1.7 Recap and Check-in

2. The Impact of Toxic Behavior at Home and Work   21
    - 2.1 How Toxicity Strains Relationships: Short- and Long-term Effects
    - 2.2 The Impact on Children by Toxic Parenting
    - 2.3 Workplace Dynamics: The Cost of Toxic Interactions
    - 2.4 Emotional Disconnection: The Unseen Consequence
    - 2.5 Recap and Check-in

3. Digging Deeper into Root Causes   35
    - 3.1 Unpacking Learned Behaviors
    - 3.2 Insecurity as a Driver
    - 3.3 The Role of Elevated Self-Perception

3.4 Insensitivity and Apathy Unveiled
3.5 Stress, Burnout, and Their Hidden Influence
3.6 Recap and Check-in

4. Overcoming Skepticism to Welcome Personal Change   49
    4.1 Debunking Myths: What Self-Development Really Means
    4.2 Logical Reasoning: The Science of Personal Change
    4.3 Finding Motivation: Personal Reasons for Change
    4.4 Overcoming Fear of Change: Embracing the Unknown
    4.5 Recap and Check-in

5. Looking Inward for Skeptics   60
    5.1 The Bias Blind Spot: Uncover What You Can't See
    5.2 The Personal SWOT Analysis
    5.3 Techniques for Looking Inward
    5.4 Emotional Vocabulary Expansion: Name the Unnamable
    5.5 Identify Your Triggers to Manage Them
    5.6 Cognitive Dissonance: Are Feelings of Hypocrisy Making You Toxic?
    5.7 Recap and Check-in

6. Improve Communication Skills   84
    6.1 Listening vs. Hearing
    6.2 Assertive vs. Aggressive: Find the Right Balance
    6.3 Feedback: Giving and Receiving without Defensiveness
    6.4 Non-verbal Cues: The Unspoken Language of Interaction
    6.5 Overcome the Echo Chamber
    6.6 Recap and Check-in

7. Manage Conflict Constructively   97
    7.1 Strategies for De-escalation: Keep Cool in Heated Moments
    7.2 Identifying the Real Issues Behind Surface Conflicts
    7.3 The Role of Compromise
    7.4 Collaborative Problem Solving: A Win-Win Approach

7.5 Set Boundaries for Healthy Relationships
7.6 Turn Disagreements into Opportunities
7.7 Recap and Check-in

8. EI and Empathy: Reality Behind the Buzzwords — 111
   8.1 Build Social Skills to Banish Toxic Behaviors
   8.2 Practical Steps to Understand People
   8.3 Empathy Gap: Learn to See Beyond Your Perspective
   8.4 Emotional Labor: The Work of Supporting Other People's Feelings
   8.5 Emotional Regulation Techniques
   8.6 Recap and Check-in

9. Digital Communication and AI Impact — 123
   9.1 The Role of Digital Communication in Modern Toxicity
   9.2 Navigate Online Interactions with Tact and Understanding
   9.3 AI for EI: Humanizing Technology
   9.4 Manage Digital Burnout: Set Boundaries in Your Connected World
   9.5 Recap and Check-in

10. Persevere to Thrive — 135
    10.1 Take on Challenges with Perseverance
    10.2 Overcome Resistance to Change
    10.3 The Role of Feedback Loops in Personal Development
    10.4 Leverage Mistakes as Learning Opportunities
    10.5 The Long-term Benefits of Continually Improving
    10.6 Recap and Check-in

Conclusion — 148

Appendix 1: Follow-Up Exercises — 150

Appendix 2: Lists — 156

Endnotes — 167

References	171
Other Books by Delia Sikes	178

INTRODUCTION

You know that moment when an inappropriate comment in a meeting sends the room into an awkward silence? Or when your partner gives you that look after you've made a joke that didn't land well, the one that says, "Seriously? Again?" These are the everyday moments when toxic behavior sneaks into our lives like an uninvited guest. It's subtle, often unintentional, and yet, it's everywhere.

Toxic behavior has become a silent epidemic in our personal and professional spaces. Approximately 2 out of every three people have faced toxic behavior at work.[1] At home, it's even more widespread. It seeps into relationships, masquerading as sarcasm, indifference, or that infamous excuse, "I'm just being honest." We often don't recognize it as toxic, or worse, we don't want to.

I've been there. I've wrestled with my tendencies to be a jerk. (That could have been me in the image above.) My consultation and process improvement background taught me a lot about systems and processes, but my real education came from life: those uncomfortable moments that make you wonder why people are upset with you. That's why I'm interested in this topic and want to share it with you.

So, what exactly is toxic behavior? It's more than just having a bad day. It's a pattern of actions or words that harm others or ourselves. It can be a snide remark, the "silent treatment," or constant criticism. Psychologically, it's often tied to insecurity, stress, learned behaviors, or, in my case, all three. Recognizing these patterns is the first step in breaking them.

Think about your daily interactions. How do your words and actions affect those around you? Are you helping or hurting the environment you're in? This exploration is about becoming the best version of yourself, not just for you but everyone in your orbit.

You might think, "I'm not toxic; these people are just overreacting," and you wouldn't be alone in that thought. It's a natural defense mechanism, and it's what I thought. We all bristle at the suggestion that we might be part of the problem. But being defensive doesn't mean you're unwilling to make a few changes. It simply means you haven't yet seen the whole picture objectively, and that's okay.

In this book, we'll explore different aspects of toxic behavior, common traits, effects, and potential root causes. You'll learn to recognize these in others and yourself. Yes, it can get a bit uncomfortable, but discomfort is just growing pains in disguise.

No one wants you to undergo a blatantly obvious personality transplant, where people ask, "Who are you, and what happened to the person we used to know?" So, we'll explore ways to change with simple steps that don't feel awkward or fake.

Now, I get it; you're skeptical. You want evidence-based, logical solutions, not touchy-feely exercises that make your eyes roll. This book contains practical advice grounded in research. **You won't find exercises or pop psychology buzzwords** in this book, only straightforward language and things to think about. (If you really want exercises, they're in Appendix 1.)

We'll also tackle modern influences like digital communication and AI. Let's face it, technology can both help and hinder our interactions. Understanding these factors is key to navigating today's complex social landscapes.

A bit more about me: I'm Delia Sikes. I've spent years consulting in systems development and process improvement while focusing on change management, emotional well-being, and personal growth. I believe in the importance of people connections to living a happy life, and I'm here to guide you through this journey.

Change is hard, but it's possible. Imagine a world where workplaces thrive on collaboration and mutual support and homes are safe places for relaxation, understanding, and love. This isn't just wishful thinking; it's achievable. With the right guidance and a bit of courage, you can change your story one step at a time.

Are you willing to explore the impact your actions have on other people? Then, let's get started on the road to a healthier, happier life. I promise it's going to be worth it.

CHAPTER 1

RECOGNIZE TOXIC BEHAVIOR

Have you ever had one of those days when you walk into the office and instantly feel the tension? Maybe it's because of your sour coworker who always has a sarcastic remark ready, or perhaps it's the manager whose presence seems to drain the joy from the room. It's funny how these behaviors can sneak up on us, turning a perfectly fine work environment into a simmering pot of discontent.

Recently, at a family gathering, I watched Aunt Laura make one of her classic passive-aggressive digs about Uncle Bob's cooking on the grill. Perhaps she was jealous of the attention he was getting and wanted to take it down a notch. We usually laugh off such a comment to break the discomfort, but it's ironic how we can be blind to our own brand of toxicity, even when it's mirrored by someone else right in front of us.

We all have these moments, whether at work or home, when our behavior might tiptoe into toxic territory without realizing it. The fact is that **toxic behavior isn't always about malicious intent**. Sometimes, it's about habit, learned responses, or even stress management that has gone wrong. Recognizing these traits is the first step in ditching them.

> Toxic behavior isn't always about malicious intent.

1.1 Defining Toxicity: What It Is and What It Isn't

Let's define what makes behavior toxic in the first place. You're in a meeting, and that one colleague (let's be honest, it could be you) is constantly negative, shooting down ideas before they have a chance to breathe. That's **Persistent Negativity**, a hallmark of toxic behavior, and a slow poison for team morale.

The same goes for **Manipulative Communication Tactics**, where someone twists words or situations to control the outcome. It's not about open dialogue; it's a one-way street to frustration.

Next is the chronic **Failure to Respect Boundaries**. This one's sneaky because it often hides under the guise of "being helpful" or "just checking in." But when you cannot relinquish control and trust other people, or you continually overstep, it's a toxic dance that erodes trust and autonomy.

You may pass off your micromanagement as helpfulness, management, or a seemingly harmless touch-base. But over time, your constant second-guessing of someone's abilities chips away at their confidence, creating an environment where nobody feels safe to do their best, learn, and grow.

These behaviors don't just live in a vacuum; they have real consequences. In the workplace, toxicity can lead to decreased morale. In 2022, a poll of 1300 employees found that 64% had faced toxic workplace behavior.[2]

At home, it erodes the very foundation of trust, turning what should be a sanctuary into a battlefield of stress and anxiety. Relationships become strained, stress levels skyrocket, and before you know it, you're living in a perpetual state of tension.

Myths

Let's dispel some myths.

- **Sarcasm** isn't always as harmless as it seems. While it might feel like a witty retort, it often masks deeper issues and can hurt more than it amuses. A single sarcastic response can be an effective way to call out someone else's toxic behavior, but the repetitive use of sarcasm when inappropriate can become toxic.

- **Assertiveness** is *not* toxic behavior. It's about expressing needs clearly, not bulldozing over others' feelings. Misunderstandings here can lead people to hold back or lash out.

See More Clearly

How do you know if a particular behavior is toxic? Ask yourself whether any of these three questions can be answered "yes."

1. Does it repeatedly harm other people?
2. Is it intended to control or manipulate?
3. Does it consistently breach mutual respect?

These questions form a basis for evaluating actions, helping you see beyond the surface and identify the true impact of your behavior. Recognizing these patterns is the first step toward creating healthier environments for you and those around you.

1.2 Spotting the Red Flags: Common Toxic Behaviors at Work

People prone to toxic behavior don't wear a badge that says "Toxic person, avoid contact," so spotting toxicity requires that you evaluate behavior.

Detecting **passive-aggressive behavior** is like trying to catch smoke with your bare hands. It's subtle **sarcasm**, often wrapped in a thin layer of **humor** or disguised as harmless banter.

- You're at the office, and someone responds to a direct question with, "Oh, I didn't realize you needed me to actually do that." They imply that they didn't do the work, although perhaps they did it. It's an underhanded dig showing they're in control and don't submit to your authority. It's wrapped in a smile and leaves everyone scratching their heads.

- You're in a meeting, and a team member throws out a sarcastic remark about deadlines, complete with a smirk. Everyone laughs, giving that team member the joy of briefly owning the room, but the project manager feels the sting. A clever sarcastic response can put the guilty party in their place. However, repetitive sarcasm that loses its humor often undermines team dynamics by sowing seeds of doubt and skepticism.

Deliberate procrastination on team projects is another sneaky way passive-aggression rears its head. The colleague who drags their feet, making you question their commitment, might be exhibiting deliberate procrastination.

Then there's the **veiled criticism, masked as a joke**. These actions slowly erode trust and collaboration, leaving the team fragmented and frustrated.

Let's not forget the office **bully**. Unlike the schoolyard version, this adult bully usually has an office and a title. They use intimidating body language, towering over you in meetings or leaning in just a little too close. They might publicly belittle coworkers, making snide remarks about their performance, appearance, or worse.

Their favorite pastime seems to be undermining people's work, often in a way that's just subtle enough to dodge formal reprimands but blatant enough to make the victim feel small. The emotional and psychological impact on victims is strong, leading to decreased productivity and heightened stress. It's a toxic cocktail that no one ordered, but everyone must drink.

There are the **chronic complainers**. You know the type; they could find a cloud in every silver lining. Their constant negativity becomes a black hole, sucking the energy out of any room. They are frequently lamenting without any intention of finding solutions.

These individuals disrupt meetings with personal grievances, turning every team discussion into a therapy session. Morale tanks and productivity takes a nosedive. Countering this behavior requires a delicate touch, often involving really listening paired with redirection toward constructive solutions.

Then there's **the constant need for validation**. Think of that friend who keeps fishing for compliments or that colleague who wants endless attention for their contribution. In cases of true insecurity, this behavior is a problem different from toxicity. However, when a person repeatedly wants to be acknowledged as the hero for "saving the day," their over-the-top desire for attention is exhausting. These interactions can drain a room faster than you can say "meeting adjourned."

Defensiveness is a classic shield against feedback. Someone offers feedback about a suggestion, and the walls go up faster than you can blink. "Well, I only said that because you..." often marks the start of a defensive spiral. This defensiveness is frequently seen in team meetings when people critique a team member's work. Instead of listening, they go on the attack, deflecting blame and shutting down productive conversation.

Finally, we have the **manipulators**. They're the chess players of the office, always two steps ahead, withholding information to gain an advantage. While some manipulation can have positive intent and outcome, is the harmful manipulators we're talking about. They play colleagues against each other, creating a web of confusion and mistrust.

Their tactics can seem innocuous at first, such as little omissions here and slight exaggerations there, but over time, they corrode the fabric of teamwork. Trust becomes a rare commodity, and collaboration falters as employees become wary of sharing information or ideas.

The Commute To and From Work

Don't forget about explosive anger exhibited by drivers, called **Road Rage**. It typically involves aggressive or hostile actions that can endanger others and contribute to a negative and harmful environment. Sure, we all express anger under our breath at inconsiderate drivers. However, road rage behaviors like shouting out an open window, rude gestures, or even physical threats and assaults, are manifestations of anger and frustration that negatively impact everyone involved.

A Pause for Thought

Take a moment to think about your workplace. Consider these behaviors to identify any you've experienced or instigated.

- Sarcastic or critical remarks disguised as jokes that lack humor
- Deliberate procrastination affecting team projects
- Bullying characterized by intimidation or belittling
- Chronic complaining without looking for solutions
- Seeking praise or validation, for attention or reassurance

- Defensive reactions to constructive feedback
- Manipulative tactics like withholding information

Think about your commute to and from work. Have you experienced or instigated aggressive Road Rage?

SEE MORE CLEARLY

So, how do you spot these traits before they spiral out of control?

- Start by writing things down on paper or in an online file. Jot down instances when interactions leave you or others feeling uneasy or frustrated. Notice any patterns across the interactions: who was involved, what was said, and how it made individual people feel. These notes can give you insights into recurring toxic behaviors.

- Get honest feedback from a trusted peer. Ask them to share their observations about your interactions. It takes courage to open yourself up to critique, but it's worth it for its clarity. Awareness is the first step to change, and sometimes, it takes an outside perspective to see clearly.

Recognizing these behaviors is the first step in addressing them. It's not about pointing fingers but understanding the dynamics contributing to a toxic work environment. Once you see the patterns, you can start making positive changes.

1.3 FAMILY DYNAMICS AND HIDDEN TOXICITY

Families can be where love and chaos collide, often leaving us scratching our heads and wondering how on earth we got here. It's where emotional manipulation can sneak in almost unnoticed, like a cat rubbing past your leg.

- **Guilt-tripping** is the art of making you feel bad. You might hear, "I guess I'll just do everything around here," a ploy to get help with chores. (In my family growing up, we heard, "I shouldn't have to ask for help or tell you what I need done; you should know what needs to be done and just do it.") It might be "Who knows how much longer Grandma will be with us," shaming you for not visiting your grandmother more often.

An occasional use of guilt-tripping can be warranted and effective; it's the repetitive use that becomes toxic.

- **The silent treatment** is that time-honored tradition of communication breakdowns. Nothing says, "I'm upset," like the awkward silence echoing through a family gathering. People use these tactics to control or influence others, leaving us feeling like we're walking on eggshells, desperate to please or appease. It's an emotional tug-of-war, where the prize is often your peace of mind. Granted, in some scenarios it can be better to be silent than argumentative. However, what becomes toxic is repeatedly using the silent treatment as a guessing game to hint that something is wrong.

- **Blame shifting** and **deflection** are the magician acts of family dynamics. When faced with an issue, some family members are experts at redirecting the blame on someone else. "It's not my fault we're late again. If you hadn't taken so long to get ready..." or "I was waiting on you. I didn't know you were already outside; you didn't tell me." Does that sound familiar? We're not talking about shifting blame when appropriate. The toxic behavior is using blame shifting repeatedly to avoid accountability.

- **Minimizing personal faults** by **exaggerating others' shortcomings** is another classic move. It's a way of avoiding responsibility and keeping the spotlight off your mistakes. This tactic damages trust and breeds resentment, as no one likes being the scapegoat in a family drama.

- An **overbearing** family member is a person who insists on dictating family decisions without considering input from others, often pushing for adherence to traditions that feel more like shackles than celebrations. This person might be a parent who insists on Sunday dinners at 5 PM sharp, and anyone who suggests a change will regret it.

These controlling behaviors may stem from a well-intentioned desire to maintain family cohesion, but they often stifle individual autonomy and breed resentment. It's hard to feel like yourself when you're constantly trying to fit into someone else's mold.

- **Defensiveness** may manifest as an argument over dishes that spirals into a debate about who has done more housework in the last decade. It's like trying to hold a conversation with an angry goose; nothing gets through, and everyone walks away frustrated.

These dynamics can turn a loving family into a battleground of emotions, leaving you feeling drained and misunderstood. However, spotting these behaviors is the first step to regaining control. The long-term damage to relationships can be significant, creating distance and distrust where you once were close.

Change is possible, even within the most entrenched family dynamics. It's about recognizing patterns and deciding not to participate in the same old dance. It starts with awareness, courage, and the willingness to set boundaries.

1.4 Bias-Driven Microaggressions: Subtle Yet Harmful

Imagine sitting in a group discussion where the conversation flows smoothly until someone says, "You're really articulate for someone from your background." Wow. Those seemingly innocuous comments pack a punch, stereotyping a class of people and leaving the recipient stuck between a compliment and an insult.

Microaggressions are those subtle slights, often unintentional, that slip into our everyday interactions, driven by **implicit biases** and **unconscious stereotypes**. They manifest in ways that make the listener wonder if they're reading too much into it, but the sting is real. It could be an insensitive joke passed around the workplace. It could be an off-hand comment about someone's capabilities based on their appearance, like in the movie "Erin Brockovich." We've all heard them and probably delivered them without a second thought.

Recognizing these bias-driven microaggressions requires an unbiased observer.

- Imagine a team meeting where someone constantly interrupts the only woman present, perhaps because they assume she's less knowledgeable. Or consider a scenario where people make assumptions about a colleague's technical skills based solely on their age or ethnicity. These are not just isolated incidents; they accumulate in the presence of complicit silence and create a sense of exclusion in the marginalized person. They contribute to a workplace where some voices are heard louder than others, not because of merit but because of unconscious bias.

- At home, it might involve assuming who should manage the finances based on gender norms without regard to skill levels, interests, or an openness to shared responsibilities. The damage of this toxic exclusion is why we should acknowledge these patterns and work toward breaking them.

The impact of microaggressions runs deep, especially for those in frequently marginalized categories of people. The cumulative effect of these slights erodes self-esteem and leads to an environment full of tension and division. It's like being part of a club where you're not quite welcome.

- Targeted individuals may start feeling isolated, questioning their value and even their place in a professional setting. This sense of alienation can affect their mental health, leading to stress and anxiety.

- It doesn't affect just that person; it chips away at group cohesion, making collaboration feel more like a battleground than a team effort.

- When people feel marginalized, innovation and morale take a nosedive, the dysfunction constrains work projects to a level of success that's potentially inferior to their potential, and everyone is left worse off.

These behaviors don't spring from nowhere. They're rooted in societal norms and biases that have been around for generations. Cultural stereotypes perpetuated by the media play a significant role in promoting institutionalized discrimination, which seeps into our everyday lives. It's like an iceberg where the visible part is just the tip. The real bulk lies beneath the surface, unseen yet ominous. But here's the silver lining: by being aware, we can start to dismantle these biases.

Addressing microaggressions requires intentional action. Encouraging open discussions about these topics can promote a more receptive environment where everyone feels heard and respected. It's about creating spaces where people can share their experiences without fear of dismissal. So, let's start the conversation.

1.5 Gaslighting and Its Consequences

Gaslighting is like a mind game that nobody signed up for. It's a form of sadistic manipulation where someone makes you question your perception of reality. Imagine you're standing next to a pot of boiling water in a kitchen, and someone insists the water's ice cold. Over time, if you hear it enough, you might start doubting your senses, wondering if you've lost touch with reality.

This psychological trickery can lead to self-doubt and confusion, as you're constantly second-guessing yourself. It's not just the occasional mind slip; it's a deliberate tactic to undermine your perception of what is the truth.

The signs of gaslighting can be subtle, but once you know what to look for, they become obvious.

- Frequent **denial of factual events** is a big red flag. It's when someone blatantly contradicts your recollection of an event, insisting that what happened didn't happen. This discrepancy isn't just about a difference in perspective; it's a persistent refusal to acknowledge reality.

- Another common tactic is **minimizing the victim's feelings**, dismissing them as overreactions or signs of being overly sensitive. The classic response, "You're just being dramatic," or "You're making a big deal out of nothing," leaves you feeling invalidated and alone.

- Gaslighters often use phrases and strategies that shift narratives, such as "You're imagining things" or "I was just joking," keeping the other person off-balance.

- They might insist on their version of reality, saying, "I never said that," repeatedly denying any wrongdoing, or belittling your concerns with, "You're overreacting." It's as if they're writing a script, and you're just an actor, unsure of your lines or what transpired in the previous scene.

- Gaslighting at home is another beast entirely. It's not just denying events that have occurred but twisting facts so that you start to question your own reality. Remember that time you were sure you left the keys on the counter, but somehow, they ended up in the fridge? According to your spouse, you're just being forgetful. But gaslighting is more than just misplaced keys; it's a deliberate attempt to confuse you and make you doubt your perceptions, leaving you feeling like you're losing your grip on reality. It can erode your confidence and self-worth, making you reliant on the person twisting the narrative. It's a psychological game where the rules keep changing, and you're always just a step behind.

Unfortunately, a person who is confused might accuse others of gaslighting when it's not true. "Gaslighting" has become a popular accusation. A perpetrator has to be pretty sadistic to use this tactic, so it's best to avoid accusations of gaslighting until you have documented evidence with witnesses. It's more important for our purpose that we understand the concept.

I experienced a form of gaslighting at a job I loved, when I became burned out and displayed toxic behaviors. The management team used this disorienting behavior to get me to quit, and after I left, it took me a year to recover from the psychological trauma.

The mental health impact of gaslighting is devastating.

- It gnaws away at your self-esteem and confidence, leaving you a shell of your former self.

- The erosion of self-trust is particularly damaging; when you can't trust your mind, you wander through life without a compass.

- Anxiety and depression often set in as you struggle to find solid ground. The constant doubt can feel like heavy fog, obscuring your judgment and sapping your energy.

- You might call in sick to work (as I did) and withdraw from social interactions because you fear judgment or further manipulation.

To combat gaslighting, the victim needs to build an arsenal of strategies.

- Keep a detailed record of events. Write down conversations and interactions as they occur. This listing is your anchor, a tangible reminder of reality when your memory feels shaky.

- Get support from a trusted person who can provide perspective and validation. Having someone confirm your experiences can be incredibly stabilizing, reminding you that you're not alone in this battle.

- Surround yourself with allies who bolster your confidence and help you see the truth.

A Pause for Thought

Are You Experiencing Gaslighting?

- Have you ever been told that your memory of an event is wrong despite being certain of your recollection?

- Do you often feel you need to apologize for your feelings or reactions?

- Have you noticed patterns where someone consistently dismisses your concerns as insignificant?

If you answered "yes" to any of these questions, consider talking to a trusted friend or therapist about your experiences.

A Pause for Thought

Recognizing gaslighting in your own actions can be an eye-opener. Have you done something like put your spouse's keys in the refrigerator, thinking it would be funny? It requires a willingness to examine past conversations for signs of manipulation.

- Think about those moments when you might have shifted the narrative, perhaps saying, "I never said that" when you did, or dismissing someone with, "You're just being too sensitive." Often, these phrases serve as shields, protecting us from facing uncomfortable truths about our behavior.

- If you're unsure whether you crossed the line, then imagine the same scene without you, as if another person was saying your lines. Do their words make you question their truthfulness?

- Getting outside perspectives can also provide clarity. Friends and family who are uninvolved in your interactions can offer insights into how your actions might be perceived. They can help you spot patterns that you might miss, providing a mirror to your behavior.

Recognizing these cues is only part of the battle. Once you see them in yourself, you have the power to change.

MAKE IT BETTER

Correcting your gaslighting behavior begins with a commitment to open communication.

- Start by validating people's experiences and acknowledging their feelings without judgment or dismissal.

- If past manipulations have occurred, own up to them and apologize sincerely. For example, "Remember when I claimed I never agreed to go to that reception? The truth is, I said I'd go but wished I hadn't because I wanted to watch the game. I'm sorry I misled you."

- It's not about beating yourself up for past mistakes but about taking responsibility and rebuilding trust.

- Open dialogue is key, where both parties feel heard and respected, creating a foundation for healthier interactions.

Creating an environment where people feel safe to express themselves without fear of being misled can improve relationships. It's about building trust and understanding, where everyone's reality is acknowledged. This shift doesn't happen overnight, but with intention and effort, it's achievable.

1.6 UNDERSTANDING TOXIC POSITIVITY AND ITS IMPACT

Imagine you're having one of those days: traffic was bad, your coffee spilled, and you missed a work deadline. You're venting to a friend, hoping for compassionate understanding, when they hit you with, "Well, everything happens for a reason." You pause, forcing a smile, but inside, you scream, "OMG, not now!"

This is **toxic positivity**, the idea that no matter how dire a situation is, you should always look on the bright side, brushing aside any negative emotions. While the intent might be good, insisting on relentless positivity can come off as dismissive, leaving people feeling isolated. If your response to the death of your coworker's dog is "you can get another one," that dismisses their sense of loss rather than sympathizing with it.

The effects of toxic positivity go beyond single experiences, subtly undermining mental health and relationships. Imagine constantly being told to "cheer up" without anyone genuinely listening to your concerns. It's like being told to enjoy swimming in the lake when you're drowning and need a life raft.

When a toxically positive person dismisses a person's struggles with a casual phrase like, "It'll get better," it can feel like that person's pain isn't valid or worth acknowledging. Over time, this can lead to increased feelings of isolation for the victim. They might bottle up their emotions, withholding them from the toxically positive person due to fears of judgment or trivialization. If they don't find a sympathetic listener, the bottled-up emotions build a wall that blocks genuine support. Relationships suffer as the lack of authentic connection creates a rift.

In our everyday lives, toxic positivity often sneaks in under the guise of well-meaning advice.

- Suppose you have a coworker who just got passed over for a promotion for which they've worked tirelessly. Instead of acknowledging their disappointment, they're told, "Something better is around the corner!" While it sounds encouraging, it dismisses their hard work and the sting of rejection.
- Similarly, hearing "There are plenty of fish in the sea!" during a tough breakup can feel more like a brush-off than comfort.

Though intended to uplift, these platitudes are a barrier to genuine understanding.

MAKE IT BETTER

So, what's the alternative? It starts with actively listening. Instead of cheerleading with a positive spin, jumping to solutions, or even blaming them for their misfortune, take a moment to truly hear what someone is saying. It doesn't matter whether you agree with them or think they're overreacting. Validate their feelings with a simple acknowledgment, such as "That sounds really tough."

It's okay to feel a range of emotions, from joy to sadness; things don't have to be all positive. Allowing space for these negative feelings creates an environment where people feel seen and heard. It's about trading the mask of constant happiness for the richness of authentic connection. Sometimes just being there is enough.

> It doesn't matter whether you think they're overreacting. Validate their feelings with a simple acknowledgment.

1.7 RECAP AND CHECK-IN

Thinking back on what we've explored, it's clear that toxic behavior is like a chameleon: sometimes glaringly obvious, other times camouflaged in the everyday fabric of our lives. We've peeled back the layers on various forms of toxicity, from microaggressions to gaslighting and even toxic positivity, which is often a failed attempt at well-meaning support.

Though varied, these behaviors share a common thread: they corrode the foundations of trust and respect in personal and professional relationships. Whether it's the subtle sting of a backhanded compliment or the relentless cheerleader who dismisses real concerns, they have an impact. They create environments where anxiety and self-doubt thrive, leaving us questioning not only the intentions of others but our perceptions as well.

A Pause for Thought

As we've journeyed through these topics, consider what this means for us personally.

- Have any of the behaviors described struck a chord?

- Did you find yourself nodding along, recognizing these traits in a colleague, a friend, or perhaps even yourself?

It's a difficult question but an important one. Awareness is the first step, and your recognition of these patterns is like turning on a light in a dim room. Only then can we see the mess and begin to clean it up. See Appendix 1 if you'd like to work through some thought-provoking questions. See Appendix 2 for summarized lists from Chapters 1-3.

Toxicity isn't just about those glaringly obvious acts of meanness; it often creeps in through overlooked habits and unchecked biases. These questions aren't about pointing fingers or assigning blame but rather about understanding that we're all capable of slipping into these patterns. The good news is we also discussed ways to recognize and address these behaviors.

Fundamentally, you want to ask whether your actions are helpful, creating connection, or harmful, creating distance. By inviting this level of thought, we can learn to recognize toxic traits in others and ourselves. It's about taking responsibility and changing how we interact with those around us.

Are there behaviors you'd like to change or relationships you'd like to mend? Remember, the goal isn't perfection; it's progress. It's about becoming more aware, more understanding, and nicer. You can start with small steps that will build to redefine the dynamics in your life.

> It's about becoming more aware,
> more understanding, and nicer.

CHAPTER 2

THE IMPACT OF TOXIC BEHAVIOR AT HOME AND WORK

Imagine you're at a family dinner, and the tension is almost as thick as Grandma's gravy. Your brother makes a jab at your dislike of certain foods, and your dad chimes in with a comment about the friends you like to spend time with. They say it's all in good humor, but you feel that lingering sting.

2.1 How Toxicity Strains Relationships: Short- and Long-term Effects

Toxic behavior, whether intentional or not, can create ripples that disturb even the calmest of waters. These everyday interactions, often dismissed as harmless banter, can erode the very fabric of your relationships, both at home and at work.

See More Clearly

Let's dive into how these toxic actions can lead to friction and conflict, making a person tiptoe through a minefield. When someone consistently criticizes or belittles you, it doesn't just roll off your back like water off a duck. Instead, it smolders, sparking arguments that flare up like a match to kindling.

It's like a never-ending cycle where heightened emotional tension and anxiety become unwelcome guests at every gathering. You might find yourself snapping over minor inconveniences, fueled by an undercurrent of unresolved resentment. It's exhausting. You're constantly walking on eggshells, waiting for the next verbal bomb to drop. (I grew up in an environment like this.)

Sustained toxic behavior is like a cancer growing into long-term damage. It can irreparably harm relationships, gradually chipping away at trust and intimacy. Over time, the person you once confided in becomes a stranger standing on the other side of an emotional canyon you never intended to create. This emotional distancing often leads to estrangement, where conversations become strained, and silence fills the spaces once occupied by laughter and shared secrets. It's a gradual process, like putting on weight, only this time, your relationships lose their vibrancy.

Similarly, friendships with long-standing histories aren't immune. A friend's sarcastic digs or passive-aggressive comments can tarnish years of camaraderie, leaving both parties wondering where things went wrong.

MAKE IT BETTER

So, how do we mend these strained relationships? It starts with open, honest communication. Instead of deflecting blame or avoiding the topic altogether, imagine that you sit down with your friend or family member and lay it all out on the table. It's not easy, I'll admit, but it's essential. When *both people* are willing to be honest and receptive, then apologizing for past behaviors and genuinely listening to each other's perspectives can work wonders. Sometimes, a simple "I'm sorry, I didn't realize" can open doors to healing you never thought possible.

Professional counseling or mediation can also play a pivotal role in repairing relationships. A neutral third party can help both sides navigate their emotions and find common ground. It's like having a guide through a dense forest of misunderstandings, helping you find your way back to each other. It feels awkward at first, but the benefits far outweigh the discomfort. After all, isn't it worth a bit of vulnerability to regain the closeness you once cherished?

> Counseling feels awkward at first,
> but the benefits outweigh the discomfort.

Addressing toxic behavior requires more than just patching up the cracks. It's about rebuilding the foundation on which your relationships stand, ensuring it's strong enough to weather future storms. As you consider this journey, remember that change doesn't happen overnight. It takes time, patience, and a willingness to confront the parts of ourselves we'd rather ignore or dismiss as bygones. But once you start, you'll find that the rewards, a stronger connection, a deeper understanding, and a more harmonious life, are well worth the effort.

A PAUSE FOR THOUGHT

Are Your Relationships Affected by Toxicity?

- Do you avoid specific conversations with loved ones due to fear of conflict or to avoid looking vulnerable?

- Have you noticed a decline in communication or trust with someone close to you?

- Are recurring arguments that seem unresolved leaving a lingering sense of tension?

If so, then consider the strategies we've discussed to repair and strengthen these connections.

2.2 The Impact on Children by Toxic Parenting

Parent-child relationships are more vulnerable to toxicity than others. When a parent persistently invalidates a child's feelings or choices, it can create a chasm that might take years to bridge or be irreparable.

The child grows up feeling unheard, leading to a cycle of detachment and misunderstanding. Even worse, that child doesn't learn what healthy relationships look like, so they perpetuate the toxic behavior in their adult life.

This toxic environment is often labeled a **dysfunctional home**. It is characterized by patterns of negative, harmful, or neglectful interactions among family members that impede the emotional, psychological, and often physical development of the children involved. Such environments lack the necessary conditions for secure attachment, healthy emotional expression, and supportive family dynamics.

Characteristics

Here are key characteristics of a dysfunctional home driven by toxic parent behavior:

- **Lack of Emotional Support**: Parents may be emotionally unavailable or inconsistently responsive, leaving children feeling neglected or emotionally abandoned.

- **Inappropriate Boundaries**: Toxic parents may blur the lines between child and adult responsibilities, imposing adult expectations on children, disclosing too much personal information, or looking to the child for emotional support, often referred to as parentification.[3]

- **Manipulation**: Parents might use guilt, fear, or obligation to control their children's behaviors and decisions. They might employ tactics such as gaslighting to make children doubt their own perceptions and feelings.

- **Abuse**: This can be physical, emotional, or psychological, including verbal abuse (insults, belittling), physical harm, or severe punishments that are disproportionate to the child's behaviors.

- **High Conflict and Instability**: A home environment with frequent yelling, fighting, or tension between parents or between parents and children creates a sense of insecurity and fear.

- **Criticism and Neglect**: Children may face constant criticism, unrealistic expectations, and general neglect of their basic emotional and physical needs.

- **Conditional Love**: Affection and approval are based on the child's performance or behavior, leading to an unstable sense of self-worth that is highly dependent on meeting parental standards.[4]

CONSEQUENCES

Growing up in a toxic household impacts a child's emotional, cognitive, and physical development.

The **emotional and psychological impacts** of toxic parenting are regrettable.

- **Low Self-Esteem**: Constant criticism or neglect can lead children to believe they are unworthy of love and respect.

- **Anxiety and Depression**: Living in a chronically stressful environment can result in anxiety disorders or depressive states in children.

- **Difficulty Forming Relationships**: Exposure to dysfunctional interactions can impair a child's ability to form healthy relationships later in life.

- **Chronic Stress and Trauma**: Long-term exposure to a toxic environment can lead to symptoms of chronic stress and even post-traumatic stress disorder (PTSD).

This environment affects the child's **intellectual development**.

- **Impaired Cognitive Development**: High stress levels can affect brain development and impair cognitive functions.

- **Academic Struggles**: Emotional and psychological distress can distract from or deprioritize academic performance and lead to difficulties in school.

The toxic dynamics can lead to **damaging actions** by the child.

- **Behavioral Problems**: Children may exhibit aggressive, withdrawn, or disruptive behaviors as a coping mechanism.

- **Substance Use**: Adolescents in toxic households might turn to drugs or alcohol as an escape from their home life.

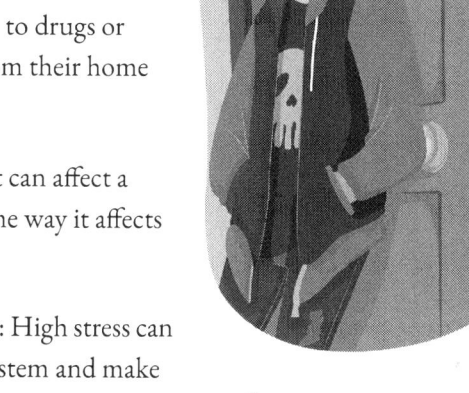

The dysfunctional environment can affect a child's physical health in the same way it affects an adult.

- **Poor Physical Health**: High stress can weaken the immune system and make children more susceptible to physical illnesses.[5]

Children raised in such environments often struggle with long-term emotional and mental health issues, such as anxiety, depression, low self-esteem, difficulty trusting people, and an overarching sense of insecurity. Without intervention, they may carry these dysfunctional patterns into adult relationships and their own parenting styles.

> Without intervention, children of toxic parents may carry these dysfunctional patterns into adult relationships and their own parenting styles.

In my dysfunctional childhood home, at least 4 of the characteristics described above applied. Since only one parent was toxic, I was fortunate not to suffer more consequences, but that was enough to influence my toxic behavior.

I remember as an adult and mother when I started taking medication for ongoing anxiety. About a week later, I gave my elementary-age children permission to do something that I had frequently denied over my anxiety that something could go wrong. They surprised me when they said, "Mom, you're being so much nicer lately!" My heart melted. I explained to them that I didn't want to be mean; it came from feeling anxious a lot. I apologized that they had to deal with that and explained that I wanted to be nicer.

Note that as they got a little older, they confessed that they were afraid of my mother because of her angry outbursts at me, but a long distance limited their exposure.

I still feel bad about not being the World's Greatest Mom that I would wish for them. But I did something right because we have good relationships in their adulthood.

This book isn't about childhood development. I included the lists above to help you realize the potential damage of toxic behavior at home, whether children are the targets or bystanders. If toxic behavior is coming from you, your partner, or both, you'll want to make changes. Do it for the sake of these young people who have been entrusted with you for nurturing into adulthood.

A Pause for Thought

- Do you respond to your children in toxic ways?

- Think about times when your anger from work, anxiety, or exhaustion might have driven you to impulsive toxic behavior at home.

- As we review types of toxic behavior in this book and their ways to "Make It Better," write down improvements you can try when communicating with your children.

2.3 Workplace Dynamics: The Cost of Toxic Interactions

You walked into the office, coffee in hand and ready to tackle the day, only to be met with the heavy atmosphere of a workplace weighed down by toxic dynamics. It's where whispers replace open conversations, and side-eye glances are the norm. Such environments do more than make

Mondays feel unbearable. They directly impact team performance and morale, wrecking productivity.

Toxic behaviors such as snarky comments, exclusion from key meetings, and a general air of disrespect chip away at collaboration and creativity. Brainstorming the next big idea is hard when you're too busy guarding your back. It's no wonder that turnover rates skyrocket in such settings. Who wants to stick around when their self-worth is constantly under attack?

This kind of churn isn't just a headache for HR; it's a financial black hole. Replacing an employee doesn't just cost time; it drains resources. The hiring process is expensive, from job postings to interviews and training. After all this effort, you still have someone new who must learn the ropes from scratch,  often leading to decreased efficiency and, you guessed it, lost revenue. It's like pouring water into a leaky bucket; no matter how much you add, the level struggles to rise.

Leadership plays a critical role in perpetuating or mitigating this toxicity. A leader who rules with fear and intimidation might think they're keeping people on their toes, but in reality, they're creating a culture of silence and resentment. Toxic leadership styles, like micromanaging every detail or making arbitrary demands, undermine team health. Employees spend more energy on appeasing the boss than doing their jobs effectively.

Conversely, effective leaders build a positive environment by promoting open communication and encouraging feedback without fear of retribution. They understand that a happy team is a productive team, (regardless of pizza or donuts in the breakroom.) These leaders create spaces where ideas flow freely and innovation thrives. It's not about ruling with an iron fist; it's about inspiring confidence and trust.

> A leader who rules with fear and intimidation creates a culture of silence and resentment. Employees spend more energy on appeasing the boss than on their jobs.

Make It Better

So, how do we turn the tide and build a healthier workplace?

- First, implement clear communication channels. When employees feel heard and valued, they're more likely to engage positively. Encouraging regular feedback loops can help air grievances before they spiral into full-blown conflicts. But it's not just about talking and listening; it's about acting on what's said.

- Another effective strategy is organizing regular team-building activities. These don't have to be the dreaded trust-fall exercises or awkward icebreakers. Think of activities encouraging bonding, like a cooking class or a group hike. When people connect outside the usual work context, they form stronger bonds that translate into better teamwork and collaboration back in the office.

2.4 Emotional Disconnection: The Unseen Consequence

You're sitting at the dinner table without a mobile phone to stare at, and it's as quiet as a library. Not a peaceful quiet, but the kind that makes you itch with unease. This is emotional disconnection, a silent saboteur in the realm of relationships.

Toxic behavior often leads to this detachment, where the heart builds a fortress as a defense mechanism. It's like when you touch something hot, and your body instinctively recoils. In relationships, this recoil manifests as suppressed emotions and the gradual withdrawal from those around you.

When someone consistently feels invalidated, they start holding back, opting to keep emotions under lock and key rather than risk further hurt. It's a survival tactic but with a steep price. Without the reassurance of emotional support and validation, even the strongest bonds can come apart.

Let's talk about what happens when emotional disconnection settles in for the long haul. It's not just a bump in the road; it's more like a wrecked car landing in a sinkhole. Mental health takes a hit, with increased risks of depression and anxiety. You can feel like a ghost in your own life, surrounded by people yet profoundly alone.

That's the kind of loneliness that emotional disconnection breeds. It's the kind that whispers nobody truly understands or cares. As isolation grows, so does the chasm between you and the people you once felt close to. It's like living in a house where the walls keep moving farther apart, and no matter how much you shout, your voice never reaches the person on the other side of the enormous room.

SEE MORE CLEARLY

Spotting emotional disconnection isn't always straightforward. It's not like searching for car keys under the sofa; it's more like trying to solve a "what's wrong with this picture?" puzzle.

- Lack of concern for people's feelings is a telltale sign. It's when someone's troubles are met with indifference or a shrug rather than a hug or a listening ear.

- Then there's the persistent emotional numbness of detachment, where you cannot summon the energy to care about things that once mattered. It's like watching a movie in black and white when you remember it being in vibrant color. The warmth of connection is replaced by a cold, clinical detachment.

Make It Better

Rebuilding emotional connections requires **paying attention to and really listening** to the other person. It's like tending to a neglected garden, focusing on what it really needs. It takes effort and patience, but the results are worth it.

- **Paying attention** is often called Mindfulness, a trendy buzzword. It means thinking about the present without letting your mind wander to other things. Concentrating on the moment allows you to truly converse with the people around you rather than getting lost in your thoughts. It's about participating emotionally, not just being physically present.

- **Really listening** to the other person is often called Active Listening, another trendy buzzword. You try to truly hear and think about what the other person says. It's about giving your full attention, not just waiting for your turn to speak. It's also about hearing what's left unsaid, picking up on the nuances that words alone can't convey.

- **Engaging in shared activities** also helps mend emotional divisions. Think of it as rekindling a fire that's only glowing embers. Activities like cooking a meal together, going for a walk, or even tackling a home project can improve connection.

These shared experiences create opportunities for conversation and laughter, slowly bridging the emotional distance. It's like weaving a tapestry, one thread at a time, until it forms a beautiful picture of the relationship you'd like to have.

> Rebuilding emotional connections requires paying attention to the other person and really listening to them.

2.5 Recap and Check-In

You've made it through a tour of toxicity's impacts at work, at home, on children, and even in the quiet spaces of your own mind. We've explored how toxic behavior isn't just those big explosive moments; it's often the subtle, insidious interactions that slowly corrode the foundations of our relationships. Toxicity can be found in those little comments or actions that initially seem harmless but gradually erode trust and create emotional distance. It's like a slow leak in a tire that eventually leaves you stranded on the side of the road, a place where no one wants to be.

Think about how toxic behaviors impact workplace dynamics. It's not just about some people making life miserable for everyone else.

- Toxicity can morph into a culture of negativity, where collaboration and creativity go to die. Imagine an office where ideas are shot down before they can even take flight, where every meeting feels like a battle rather than a brainstorming session. It's exhausting.

- It doesn't just affect morale; it also affects the financial bottom line. Companies end up losing valuable employees, spending time and money on hiring replacements, and then facing the same issues again because the underlying culture hasn't changed.

Toxic environments lead to emotional disconnection. The interactions create an environment where people put up walls, shutting down emotionally to protect themselves. This isn't just about feeling a little blue; it's a deep-seated sense of isolation that can lead to anxiety and depression. (Full confession: This is how I felt in my job when my burnout led to my toxicity, which was followed by the manager's gaslighting to get me to quit.)

Think of it like being in a crowded room but feeling utterly alone. You might find yourself going through the motions, nodding in conversations but not engaging. The warmth that once filled your interactions is replaced by a cold detachment, leaving relationships feeling hollow or non-existent.

But before you start to feel overwhelmed, remember that recognizing these patterns is a decisive first step. It's like finally seeing both the forest and the trees. Once you understand the impact of toxic behavior, you can begin to make conscious changes. Whether opening up communication lines at work or taking the initiative to reconnect with loved ones, every small step counts. It's about promoting environments where people feel safe expressing themselves and where differences are explored rather than stifled.

A Pause for Thought

Ask yourself if you have noticed these results in your own life.

- At work, is there a tense atmosphere that dampens everyone's enthusiasm?
- At home, do conversations feel like the minimum required between housemates, perhaps with tense negotiations?
- Have you found yourself emotionally checked out or noticed people around you doing the same?

These are signs that toxicity has taken its toll. Acknowledging this isn't about placing blame; it's about understanding the dynamics at play so you can shift them in a healthier direction.

As we wrap up this chapter, think about personal and professional relationships in your life.

- Where do you see the need for improvement?
- What small changes can you make to repair any damage caused by toxic interactions?

It's not about completing an overhaul overnight; it's about taking one step at a time to create a more supportive and positive atmosphere. Remember, the goal is progress, not perfection.

In the next chapter, we'll review the root causes of toxic behavior and explore how learned patterns and self-perception shape our interactions. Understanding these underlying factors will give you the tools to recognize and change the behaviors holding you back.

See Appendix 1 if you'd like to work through some thought-provoking questions.

See Appendix 2 for summarized lists from Chapters 1-3.

CHAPTER 3

DIGGING DEEPER INTO ROOT CAUSES

Have you ever caught yourself saying something and thought, "Wow, I sound just like my mom"? (I have!) It's that eerie moment when you realize the apple didn't just fall close to the tree; it stayed there.

3.1 Unpacking Learned Behaviors

The world of **learned behaviors** is where our childhood experiences and early environments play a starring role in shaping who we are today. It's like inheriting the family's fine chinaware but wishing you could swap out the pattern for something more in line with your tastes.

These behaviors have deep roots, often planted by influential figures during our formative years.

- Think about how your parents handled disagreements. Did they talk it out over a cup of coffee, yell accusations, or go silent, leaving you to guess what was wrong?
In my family, my mother yelled, my father went silent, and afterward, everyone tiptoed away, walking on eggshells. Later, we acted like nothing ever happened. There were no apologies.

- Think about the biases of your parents toward types of people based on things like class, race, or where you were from.

We soak up these attitudes and communication styles like sponges, adopting them as our own without realizing it.

The workplace is another arena where learned behaviors take the stage. Remember your first job? Fresh out of school and eager to make your mark, you likely adopted office norms like a uniform.

- You might have developed a sharp, competitive edge if the culture was cutthroat.

- If teamwork was valued, you probably learned to collaborate effectively.

- If everyone worked individually, like my first job, you may have learned a strong work ethic but not how to collaborate as a team.

These early work experiences set the tone, influencing how you interact with colleagues and handle workplace challenges. It's like learning to dance; you pick up the steps from those around you, whether they're graceful or clumsy.

Here's the bigger issue: the learned behaviors from home don't stay neatly contained at home. They spill over into work from our personal lives, often replicating family dynamics in our work relationships. It's like playing out an old script you didn't even know you'd memorized.

You may find yourself using sarcasm as a default communication style, a habit picked up from a parent who wielded it like a sword. While it might seem harmless or even clever, sarcasm can erode trust and understanding, creating a toxic interaction pattern. It's like adding a drop of vinegar to every conversation; eventually, the sweetness disappears, leaving only the sour notes.

MAKE IT BETTER

So, how do we break free from these ingrained patterns? It starts with recognizing them. Think of it as identifying weeds in a garden; you can't pull them out if you don't see them.

Thinking about yourself is necessary (which is called "self-reflection," another trendy buzzword.)

- Consider writing down details about when interactions didn't go well.
- Think about what might have triggered your potentially toxic response and note it. It could be something familiar, like a reflex learned long ago.

Once you see your pattern of using learned responses, you can become more aware of what's happening in real-time and begin to change it. It's not about erasing the past but understanding its influence and choosing a different path forward.

> Recognizing ingrained patterns is like identifying weeds in a garden. You can't pull them out if you don't see them.

GET A COACH?

Behavioral therapy can be a valuable tool in this process of change. Counseling is like having a coach guide you through the process, offering strategies to replace harmful behaviors with healthier alternatives. You can explore the origins of your learned behaviors, gaining insight into why you react the way you do.

This understanding helps you make conscious choices, turning knee-jerk reactions into thoughtful responses. It's like upgrading your operating system, allowing you to function more smoothly and effectively.

A PAUSE FOR THOUGHT

Try to identify your learned behaviors.

- Think about a recent interaction that didn't go well. What was your immediate response?
- Think about when you were growing up. Are there behaviors you see in yourself that mirror those of your parents or early caregivers?
- Consider writing down patterns you notice in your relationships. Do you see any recurring themes or triggers?

This awareness is the first step in breaking the cycle and creating healthier interactions.

3.2 INSECURITY AS A DRIVER

Insecurity can be a subtle yet pervasive root cause of toxic behavior. It often manifests as a deep-seated fear of not being good enough, which can drive individuals to adopt defensive or aggressive behaviors as protection. Imagine being in a team meeting where you feel outclassed by your colleagues' accomplishments. Instead of celebrating their success, you might minimize their achievements or redirect the focus. This isn't necessarily about overshadowing people deliberately; it's more about battling an internal narrative of inadequacy.

This kind of insecurity often stems from a lack of self-esteem, which might be influenced by previous failures or a chronic sense of underachievement. People struggling with insecurity may try to cover up their perceived deficiency by criticizing or undermining others.

For example, consider a manager who consistently micromanages their team. This behavior might not stem from a desire to control but from an insecurity about their capabilities. They might fear getting caught not knowing what's going on, so they use micromanaging to learn enough to sound knowledgeable.

Insecurity can also lead to jealousy or resentment towards other people's successes or happiness. In a work environment, this can result in a toxic atmosphere where collaborative success is overshadowed by competitive undercurrents. It's like being in a boat where instead of rowing together, some are drilling holes under their seats to sink the other people, either not realizing that the ensuing water will sink everyone or not caring.

Make It Better

Addressing insecurity involves building a culture of support and affirmation. Encouraging open communication and recognizing achievements can help build a more secure environment. Here are some practical steps:

- **Encourage personal development**: Invest in training and development programs. This will improve skills and boost confidence.

- **Promote a culture of feedback**: Implement regular, constructive feedback sessions that help individuals understand their strengths and areas for improvement without feeling threatened.

- **Recognize achievements**: Regular acknowledgment of accomplishments can reinforce a sense of competence and worth. Everyone deserves to be recognized.

3.3 The Role of Elevated Self-Perception

Have you ever met someone who enters a room and acts like they own the place? Maybe that person is you, or you've been accused of it. Elevated self-perception is that little voice whispering in your ear, telling you that you're above the fray, immune from criticism, and deserving of special treatment. It's like having an overinflated balloon of self-worth, which, if unchecked, can float you right past humility and into the stratosphere of arrogance.

When you believe you're smarter than everyone else, dismissive or arrogant behavior often follows. You might find yourself thinking, "I'm too good for this," "I know the answers better than anyone else does," or "Things would fall apart without me" (as I did,) and you tune out feedback or brush off suggestions from people as being whiny or naive. This self-view can create a chasm between you and the world, where you're perched on a pedestal of your own making. Sadly, you're more annoying than revered up there.

See More Clearly

How do you know if you're caught up in this inflated self-view?

- One telltale sign is a tendency to interrupt people, convinced that what you have to say is more important. (This got me in trouble.) You might find yourself finishing people's sentences or speaking over them in meetings, not out of malice but from a misguided belief in your superiority.

- Another indicator is a reluctance to accept feedback, especially if it challenges your self-image. Criticism feels like a personal attack, and instead of considering it, you dismiss it outright or deflect it onto someone else. This can lead to a sense of entitlement, where you expect people to cater to your needs or bend the rules in your favor.

The consequences of elevated self-perception will be damaging, often alienating you from peers who see your behavior as arrogant or rude. Even when you've done a great job on something, you won't get that "employee of the month" recognition because management can't afford to look like they're endorsing your attitude. Relationships suffer as people pull away, tired of feeling undervalued by you or ignored. You might not realize that you have alienated people until no one sits with you at the office luncheon or after-work outing.

Professional growth stalls, too, because when you're convinced that you're the best, there's little room for improvement. Opportunities slip through your fingers as colleagues and mentors hesitate to engage with someone who doesn't listen or learn. You might even decline to learn a new area because you fear you won't be as successful there as you are in this area where you perceive that you're so valuable.

Make It Better

Cultivating humility is the antidote to this inflated self-view.

- Start by getting regular feedback from peers, not just when you're required to but as something you want to do. Ask for their honest opinions and listen without rushing to defend yourself. It's about opening the door to perspectives other than your own, allowing you to see the full picture.

- Thinking about your personal shortcomings is also crucial. Take a moment to consider areas where you've fallen short or could improve. It's not about beating yourself up but embracing the reality that everyone has room to grow. This helps you build a balanced perspective of yourself, where confidence and humility coexist.

Making these changes isn't about tearing down your self-esteem. It's about planting it in reality, where you know your strengths and limitations. Imagine the benefits of being seen as approachable, as someone who values people's input and adapts to feedback.

Relationships thrive when they're built on mutual respect, and egos take a back seat to collaboration. As you cultivate humility, you'll find that the pedestal you once stood on becomes less important, replaced by a foundation of genuine connection. After all, there's more to life than being right, (a concept I've struggled with,) and sometimes, your most significant strength lies in listening, learning, and being willing to change.

> There's more to life than being right.

3.4 Insensitivity and Apathy Unveiled

There's a fine line between being direct and being insensitive. Imagine that a colleague presents their hard work in a meeting, and you barely acknowledge it, maybe just nodding and moving on to the next agenda item. It's not that you meant to be rude; you didn't see the importance of a few words of acknowledgment.

This is where insensitivity creeps in. When we overlook people's contributions or dismiss their feelings as unimportant, we contribute to a toxic atmosphere where people feel undervalued. Insensitivity in interpersonal contexts is that blind spot where empathy should be used but isn't. It's not always about being mean-spirited; sometimes, it's about not realizing that our words or actions lack the warmth and understanding that others need.

Once, when I was ordering new choir robes for our church, I overlooked the needs of a choir member who was quite large. In my mind, she was just like everyone else, and since robes are gathered and flowing, any robe should fit her. But that assumption wasn't valid, and it wasn't a compliment; it was me being insensitive to her needs.

Think about where this insensitivity and apathy might come from. For some people like me, it's rooted in past experiences, like growing up in an environment where emotions were an afterthought. Maybe you were in a household where feelings were brushed aside (e.g., "You're just overreacting ") or where emotional expression was seen as a sign of weakness (e.g., "Get over it; you're fine").

I still remember the time my parents were scolding my two brothers and me for not helping with chores. I started crying, and they asked me why. Surprised, I replied that it was because they were upset with me and I felt bad about it. They replied that I was overreacting and was just too sensitive. That left me very confused.

These early experiences act as a blueprint for handling emotions later in life. Add defense mechanisms into the mix (e.g., "Next time, I just won't say anything"), and you have a recipe for emotional distance. When life gets tough, it's easier to shut down rather than engage. It's like putting on sunglasses to block out the sun. They're useful for eye protection, but they inhibit a one-on-one conversation.

Examples of insensitivity are all around us, hiding in plain sight. Imagine a friend sharing a tough day, and your response is dismissive, "You'll get over it," or you one-up them with stories about your work. Consider a team meeting where someone raises a concern, and you brush it off with an eye roll, assuming they're overreacting.

If you realize you've done this to someone, ask yourself, "Do you really not care? Or were you not paying attention?" Apathy and insensitivity can go hand in hand, but it helps to know which is your more significant issue.

Ignoring nonverbal cues is another common trait of insensitivity. Your partner's crossed arms and tense posture may go unnoticed because you're focused on stating your viewpoint. These small missteps can lead to significant rifts in relationships. It's like missing the warning signs before a storm; the damage is done by the time you realize what's happening.

MAKE IT BETTER

So, how do we break this cycle of insensitivity and apathy? It starts with becoming more attuned to the emotions and needs of other people. Note: This may sound like touchy-feely stuff that's more trouble than it's worth, but it matters unless you live alone on an island. Connecting with people is what life is all about, so stick with me here.

- One strategy is to pay closer attention to nonverbal cues, like body language and tone of voice, which often speak louder than words. (This skill proves you're human; artificial intelligence hasn't learned to do it.)

- When someone seems off, take a moment to ask how they're doing and really listen to their response. Empathy is your best friend here, helping bridge the gap between what you see and understand.

For more techniques, look at Chapter 9, where we discuss building empathy and understanding. The goal is to change insensitivity into real concern, turning apathy into action that strengthens connections. By making this effort, we create an environment where everyone feels valued, building relationships that thrive rather than wither.

3.5 Stress, Burnout, and Their Hidden Influence

You know that kind of day when everything feels like it's teetering on the edge? Stress is that unwelcome guest that crashes the party and doesn't know when to leave. When stress levels skyrocket, our behavior can take a nosedive into toxic territory.

Imagine juggling deadlines like flaming torches while your email inbox overflows like a busted dam. It's no wonder irritability rears its ugly head as you snap at coworkers or loved ones over seemingly trivial matters. It's like your patience meter is running on fumes, and every little hiccup feels like a personal insult. This kind of stress-induced irritability can turn the most mundane situations into battlegrounds, where even a misplaced coffee cup can spark a full-blown skirmish.

See More Clearly

Recognizing stress-induced toxicity isn't always straightforward, especially when you're in the thick of it.

- One of the first indicators is frequent complaints about workload. You might find yourself constantly grumbling about the never-ending to-do list, feeling like you're trapped in a bottomless bucket of tasks. It's like a game of whack-a-mole where every task you complete spawns two more in its place. This constant overwhelmed feeling can lead to a short fuse, where you're prone to snapping at people without even realizing it. Stress and burnout to which I was too proud to succumb is what started my descent into the realm of toxic behavior.

- Another sign is the tendency to withdraw, avoiding social interactions because the effort feels like climbing a mountain on a hot day. You might notice a lack of enthusiasm for activities you once enjoyed as the weight of stress squeezes the joy out of life.

The long-term effects of burnout can be truly debilitating, both mentally and physically. It's not just about feeling tired; it's about a deep-seated exhaustion that seeps into your bones, making even the simplest tasks feel insurmountable. Job satisfaction plummets as you struggle to find meaning in your work, and the risk of chronic health issues looms large.

Relationships bear the brunt, too, as the strain of stress creates a chasm between you and your loved ones. You react to your children's needs as just more annoying tasks, and you're too tired to give them more than minimal effort. Answering questions becomes harder, like a computer with inadequate working memory. Misunderstandings about facts and emotions multiply because insensitivity and apathy become your survival mechanism. The toll on personal connections can leave both people feeling isolated and disconnected.

MAKE IT BETTER

So, how do we tackle this stress monster before it wreaks havoc?

- **Time management** strategies can make a big difference. Imagine having a clear, organized schedule that allows you to tackle tasks efficiently rather than being overwhelmed by the chaos.

- Time management includes asking your manager to lighten your workload when it has become too much, or to prioritize concurrent projects with the understanding that one will be late. It's not because you can't handle it; it's because they assigned more than anyone can reasonably complete.

- **Prioritizing tasks and setting realistic goals** can help you regain control, turning the mountain of work into a series of manageable hills.

  - With prioritization comes the need to delegate some tasks, even when you're certain that you could do them faster and better. Think of it as a learning opportunity for the delegate, and you're their teacher.

- **Relaxation** can turn things down a notch.

  - Paying attention to the present means keeping your thoughts focused on the current moment while clearing out unrelated thoughts. Doing this serves as a reset button, allowing you to step back and view stressors from a calmer perspective.

  - A deep breath in the moment of stress (my favorite) or a short walk outside can make an amazing difference by providing a much-needed pause in the whirlwind of daily life.

These practices help clarify your thoughts and reduce the grip stress has on your behavior, allowing you to respond thoughtfully instead of just reacting.

3.6 Recap and Check-in

As we wrap up this chapter, let's take a moment to think about the hidden forces that can turn us into unintentional spreaders of toxicity. We've reviewed the different root causes; each one is a potential culprit in steering our behavior off course. Whether it's the ingrained habits we've picked up from those around us, covering up insecurity, the inflated view of ourselves that blinds us to our own fallibility, or the insensitivity and apathy that creep into our interactions, each can play a significant role. Add stress to the mix, and you've got a perfect storm of factors that can harm even the best of us.

A Pause for Thought

Consider how these elements show up in your own life.

- Have you noticed patterns that echo the patterns of your childhood home, even when you swore that you'd never act like your parents?

- Do you suspect that behind your toxic responses, deep down, you might be compensating for insecurity?

- Have you dismissed a colleague's input, convinced that you already know best?

- Have you been surprised to learn that something you said offended someone because you never realized it might be offensive?

- Have you been told that your response to someone was toxic, but you don't care?

- In the hustle and bustle of daily life, have you found yourself tuning out the emotions of those around you, not out of malice but simply because you're running on empty?

These aren't character indictments but opportunities to learn and do better.

It's human nature to resist change, especially when it involves facing uncomfortable truths. But it's not about a complete overhaul, a sudden epiphany, or a "personality transplant." It's about small, intentional steps that lead to meaningful change over time.

So, as you think about your own experiences, ask yourself: Have any of these root causes hit home? Do you see yourself in the behaviors we've discussed? It's okay if the answer is yes. Recognizing these traits is the first step toward addressing them.

This chapter has been like looking in the mirror and seeing not just the reflection you're used to but the version of you that other people see.

- It's about understanding the why behind our actions, so we can start making conscious choices that align more closely with the person we want to be.

- It's about acknowledging that while we can't change the past, we can influence our future interactions, improving them one step at a time.

As you move forward, keep these insights in mind. In the coming chapters, we'll explore practical strategies to avoid these root causes, promoting a more understanding approach to our relationships. Turning awareness into action can create environments where connections can thrive.

See Appendix 1 if you'd like to work through some thought-provoking questions.

See Appendix 2 for summarized lists from Chapters 1-3.

Chapter 4

Overcoming Skepticism to Welcome Personal Change

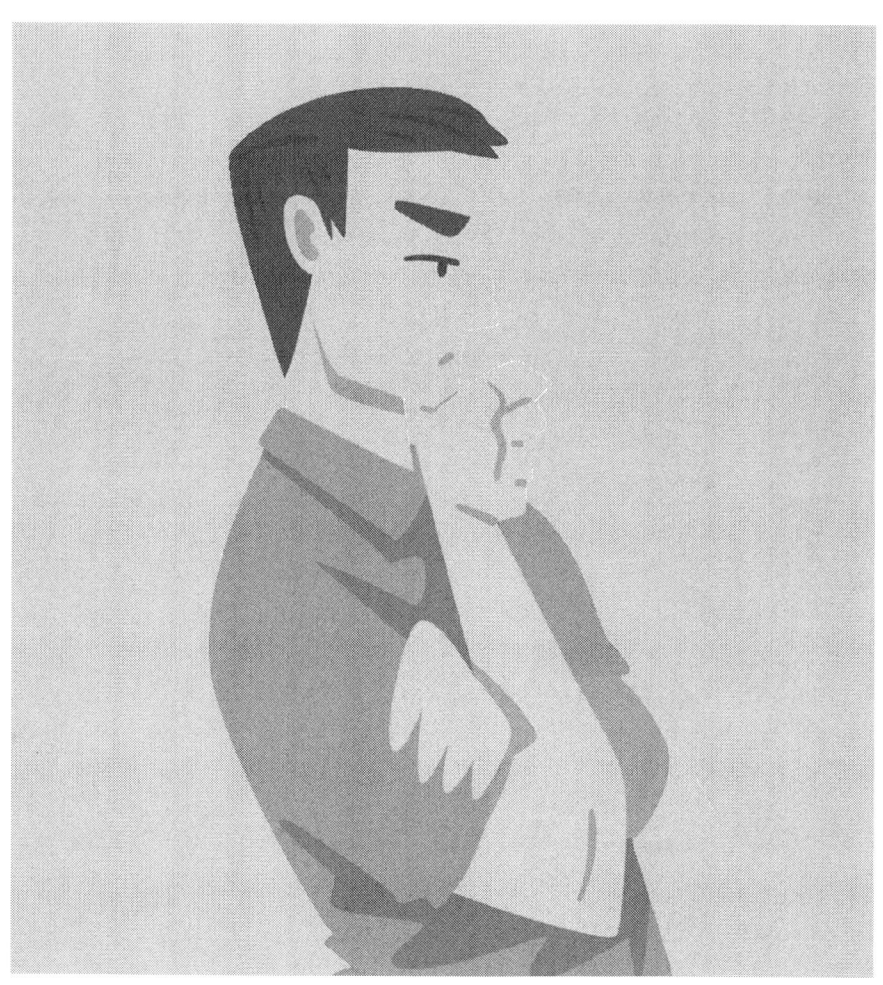

You're in a bar enjoying a beer with coworkers after a long day when you overhear a conversation. A person at the next table enthusiastically explains how a self-help book "changed their life." You visibly roll your eyes, thinking, "Here we go again ... a miracle story about positive thinking," and your teammates chuckle at your eyeroll as confirmation that they're sharing your skepticism.

Before you dismiss it entirely, let's pause and explore the world of self-improvement with a bit more refinement. It's not all rainbows and motivational posters. In fact, personal development has evolved into a diverse and evidence-backed approach to improvement that might surprise even the most skeptical among us.

4.1 Debunking Myths: What Self-Development Really Means

This book uses these terms interchangeably: self-help, self-development, personal development, self-improvement, self-care, self-guidance, self-enhancement, and self-awareness. This is to break away from the stigma and stereotypes about self-help.

Let's start with some myths that cling to self-help like gum on a shoe.

- First is the myth that self-help is only for the weak or needy. This misconception stemmed from the idea that getting help is a sign of failure, but it's not. Welcoming self-improvement or help is a sign of strength, a declaration that you're willing to invest in yourself and your future. It's like deciding to learn a new language or skill, not because you can't function without it, but because you want to.

- Second, there's the myth that all self-help advice is generic phrases to repeat, not evidence-based, effective techniques. You might visualize a sea of vague affirmations and platitudes, but the reality is far richer. Self-improvement encompasses a range of techniques based on psychology and science, offering tailored solutions for diverse needs and preferences.

The world of self-development is as varied as a buffet, catering to different tastes and styles.

- Cognitive-behavioral techniques[6] Focus on reshaping thought patterns and behaviors, addressing issues like anxiety and depression.

- Thinking only about the present (mindfulness) and thinking only about one thing or nothing (meditation) are techniques that make you more aware and calmer, reduce stress, and help you regulate your emotions.

- Professional coaching and therapy also fall under the self-improvement umbrella. They provide structured guidance and support tailored to your needs and goals.

- Whether you're receptive to a DIY approach (the "self" of self-help) or prefer interactive one-on-one sessions with a professional, help is available to improve your life.

Self-guidance is not just about feeling better temporarily; it's about making lasting changes. It means taking charge of making changes rather than waiting for change to happen. It's like being the captain of your ship, taking the wheel and charting a course toward your better world.

Self-improvement offers strategies to overcome challenges and achieve personal and professional goals. You understand yourself and others better, improving your relationships and interactions.

If you're still skeptical, let's turn to the evidence. Numerous studies support the effectiveness of self-help strategies in improving mental health outcomes.

- Cognitive-behavioral interventions can significantly reduce symptoms of anxiety and depression, offering a lifeline to those struggling with these challenges. [7]

- Cognitive Behavior Therapy can also help you overcome fears, such as fear of flying or public speaking. [7]

- Success stories abound, demonstrating how individuals have changed their lives through self-improvement, from managing stress or losing weight to improving athletic abilities.

Self-development isn't a one-size-fits-all solution. It's about embracing the tools and strategies that work for you and creating a life that aligns with your values and aspirations.

4.2 Logical Reasoning: The Science of Personal Change

Let's face it, change can be hard. But when you break it down, personal change is less about magic and more about science. At the heart of it lies neuroplasticity, which is the brain's ability to reorganize itself by forming new neural connections.[9]

Imagine your brain like a city map, with roads that can be rerouted, expanded, or even built anew. This means you can change thought patterns, behaviors, and even habits by literally rewiring your brain. Neuroplasticity is what allows us to learn new skills, recover from injuries, and adapt to life's curveballs. It's the scientific backbone that makes change possible and sustainable.

Behavioral conditioning comes into play when you think about forming new habits or breaking old ones. It's a process of learning through rewards and consequences, much like training a puppy. You reinforce the behaviors you want and gradually diminish those you don't. It's not just about willpower but understanding the mechanisms that drive your actions and using them to your advantage.

Behavioral conditioning is changing habits with rewards and consequences.

Instead of depending on willpower alone, you take advantage of your human nature to prefer something good over something bad.

In the realm of structured change, several models can guide us through the process.

- One of the most well-known is the **Stages of Change model**[10], which breaks change into manageable phases. It's a practical process that acknowledges the complexity of change and provides guidance at each step.

- It starts with pre-contemplation, where you're not even thinking about change.

- It moves through contemplation and preparation, where you start weighing the pros and cons and planning your steps.

- The action phase is where you dive in, making tangible changes.

- Finally, the maintenance stage focuses on integrating these new behaviors into your life.

- Then there's **Goal-Setting Theory**[10], which emphasizes the importance of clear, achievable objectives to motivate and guide us. Setting specific goals can change vague desires into actionable plans, much like aiming a spotlight on the path ahead, illuminating each step you need to take. It's about breaking down the journey into smaller, digestible milestones that keep you moving forward.

Let's turn to logic for those who remain skeptical about personal change.

- Although **incremental change** may seem modest at first, it accumulates over time, leading to significant improvement. Think of it as compounding interest in your personal growth bank. Each small step builds on the last, gradually reshaping your reality without overwhelming you.

- The **cost-benefit analysis** of investing in self-improvement is similarly straightforward. Consider the benefits: improved relationships, enhanced career prospects, and better mental and emotional health. Now, weigh these against the costs, such as time, effort, and discomfort. The scales tip heavily in favor of self-development, making personal growth one of the most rewarding investments you can make. It's not about drastic overhauls but about making thoughtful, strategic changes that add up over time.

Real-world examples are plentiful, showcasing how individuals have successfully navigated change through logical approaches.

- Take the story of a mid-career professional who decided to shift directions entirely. Through structured planning and goal setting, they transitioned from a corporate job to a fulfilling role in a nonprofit organization. They achieved a career shift that once seemed impossible by identifying their passions and mapping out a clear path.

- Or consider the testimonials of people who have adopted healthier lifestyles by making small, incremental changes. Typically, a person might start by replacing sugary drinks with water, then gradually introduce exercise, and before they know it, they've lost weight, gained energy, and improved their overall well-being.

These stories aren't just anecdotes; they're evidence of what's possible when logic and strategy are applied to the self-help of personal growth.

A Pause for Thought

Take a moment to visualize your path to change.

- Picture an infographic like the one shown in this book below, outlining the Stages of Change from pre-contemplation to maintenance.

- Use it as a guide to assess where you are in your own process of becoming less toxic.

- Identify which stage you're in and what steps you need to take to move forward.

- This visual map can serve as a reminder that change is a journey, with each stage offering its challenges and rewards. It's not all about the Action phase.

When viewed through the lens of science and logic, personal change becomes attainable. It's about understanding the mechanisms at play and using them to craft a life that aligns with your goals.

Stages of Change

1. PRE-CONTEMPLATION
"I don't need to change."

2. CONTEMPLATION
"Ok, maybe I do need to change."

3. PREPARATION
"So, what do I do?"

4. ACTION
"Let's do this."

5. MAINTENANCE
"I did it."

Whether you're looking to change careers, adopt healthier habits, or improve your relationships, the principles of neuroplasticity, behavioral conditioning, and structured change models offer a roadmap to guide you.

4.3 Finding Motivation: Personal Reasons for Change

Imagine waking up one morning with a clear sense of purpose, feeling the pull of something better just within your grasp. It could be the desire to mend a strained relationship or the spark of ambition urging you to climb higher in your career.

These personal motivators act like the wind in your sails, pushing you toward change.

- Improved relationships and social interactions often top the list. Who doesn't want more fulfilling connections with family, friends, and colleagues? Perhaps you've noticed a pattern of misunderstandings or want to deepen those bonds that matter most.

- Aspirations for advancement and success can be powerful drivers in the career field. The call to excel is strong whether you're eyeing that promotion or dreaming of starting your own venture.

Identifying these motivators is like tuning into your own personal radio station, catching the signals that resonate most with your heart and mind.

> Write down motivating reasons to end toxic behavior.

But let's be honest, motivation can be slippery. One moment, you're ready to conquer the world; the next, you binge-watch a series you've already seen twice.

Make It Better

So, how do you keep that fire burning?

- **Setting clear, achievable goals** is a good start. Think of them as steppingstones, each one leading you closer to your dreams. Make them specific and give yourself tangible rewards for reaching them. It's like setting up your personal treasure hunt, with each milestone offering a little prize.

- Consider creating a **Vision Board**. I know, it sounds like arts and crafts, but visualizing your goals can be incredibly motivating. A picture speaks 1000 words! Clip out images, words, or anything representing your aspirations and stick them on a board. You can also use computer apps to put them on an image for the background of your computer. Put it somewhere you'll see it daily, and let it serve as a constant reminder of where you're headed.

How can you create a Vision Board for becoming less toxic? At home, a photo collage of happy times can represent the benefits of harmony. At work, look for images of collaborative teams succeeding. No one needs to know why you've hung these collages; it can be a secret motivator.

Of course, motivation isn't just about setting goals; it's about overcoming the roadblocks that make you want to give up.

- Fear of failure is a big one. It lurks in the background, whispering doubts and what-ifs. But remember, failure isn't the enemy; it's a teacher. Each setback offers a lesson, a chance to refine your approach and try again.

- Procrastination is another sneaky motivation-killer, lulling you into a false sense of security with promises of "I'll do it later." One way to tackle it is by breaking tasks into smaller, manageable chunks, making them less daunting and more doable. It's like eating a pizza one slice at a time rather than trying to devour the whole thing.

Don't go it alone; other people can help keep you motivated.

- Building a supportive environment can make all the difference in sustaining motivation. Surround yourself with people who encourage you. A person who acts as your coach and cheerleader is great for this; they know your plan, hold you to your commitments, and praise you as you progress. (This person is also called an accountability partner, another trendy buzzword.)

- Joining teams with similar goals (support groups or communities) can also provide a sense of camaraderie. There's something powerful about connecting with other people on a similar path, sharing experiences and insights, and knowing you're not alone. These networks act as a safety net, catching you when you falter and pushing you to keep going when the going gets tough.

4.4 Overcoming Fear of Change: Embracing the Unknown

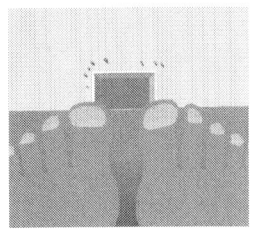

Imagine that you're standing on the edge of a diving board, toes slightly over the edge, looking down at the water below and all the tiny people nearby. That knot in your stomach? That's the fear of the unknown, a natural response to change that every one of us experiences at some point. It's not just the fear of what's to come but the uncertainty of leaving what you know behind.

Change can feel like you're losing control, disrupting the stability you've relied on. It's like swapping out your trusty old pair of jeans for a new style: exciting yet terrifying because what if they don't fit right or feel natural?

This fear often leads to anxiety, that gnawing worry about what might happen if things don't go as planned. You might find yourself stuck in a cycle of overthinking, each what-if more unnerving than the last. But, while fear is a natural part of life, it doesn't have to hold you back.

Make It Better

Managing this anxiety requires a toolbox of strategies.

- **Focus**: This strategy is to think only about the present moment, thinking about only one thing, like a leaf floating gently on a stream, or thinking about nothing. This stabilizing technique helps to calm the swirling thoughts, offering a reprieve from the chaos and giving you the clarity to navigate and move forward with a clear head.

- **Baby Steps**: Another approach is gradual exposure to new experiences. Think of it as dipping your toes into cold water before diving in. By slowly introducing yourself to new situations, you build confidence, proving to yourself that you can handle whatever change throws your way.

- **Positive Perspective**: What if you could see change not as a threat but as a positive force? It's all about perspective. Reinterpreting change as an optimistic adventure can improve your experience. It's a chance to shed old habits and reach new possibilities.

- **Flexibility**: Life rarely goes according to plan, and being able to adjust your approach in response to changing circumstances is invaluable. Think of it like a skilled sailor who adjusts their sails to catch the wind no matter the direction.

- **Recognize Progress**: Each step forward, no matter how small, is a victory worth acknowledging. Treat yourself to a little celebration, whether it's a pat on the back or a night out with friends. These moments of recognition fuel your motivation, reminding you that change is about the journey itself.

4.5 Recap and Check-in

In this chapter, we sought to debunk your skepticism about self-help (or self-improvement) by exploring science and evidence supporting its success. We looked at logical models for change that can make it more approachable.

We reviewed motivation for change and ways to keep that motivation. We explored the natural fear of change and offered strategies to manage it, encouraging you to welcome change as a positive force.

A Pause for Thought

Think about how ditching skepticism will allow you make small improvements every day, to become not just a spectator but an active participant in your own evolving story.

See Appendix 1 if you'd like to work through some thought-provoking questions.

CHAPTER 5

LOOKING INWARD FOR SKEPTICS

Have you ever driven home on autopilot, only to arrive and think, "Wait, how did I get here?" It's like your brain skips the whole journey while you're lost in thought.

5.1 The Bias Blind Spot: Uncover What You Can't See

Blind spots in our behavior are pretty much like that: unseen. They're things we don't see coming, driving us headlong into misunderstandings or conflicts. Imagine you're in a meeting, nodding along while secretly checking emails on your phone. *You* think you're multitasking like a pro, but *your colleagues* see you as disengaged or rude. Ironically, you would have judged a coworker as disengaged or rude for perusing their phone.

These blind spots, often fueled by cognitive biases[12], can hold us back from being our best selves at work and home. We think we're objective, but often we're not, thanks to the **bias blind spot**[13]. This mental hiccup causes us to see others' flaws clearly while overlooking our own because we think we're less biased than other people. This sneaky phenomenon can cause us to miss valuable opportunities for improvement.

Biases affect decisions, but they also seep into relationships and interactions. It is important to explore how your biases influence behavior.

- Maybe you're not good at public speaking, so you avoid it like the plague. But what if that's just a story you've told yourself, and you simply never learned how?

- What other stories have you told yourself that might not be true?

Recognizing these narratives is the first step toward changing them. They're like strings limiting your actions; cutting them frees you to be yourself.

See More Clearly

The tricky part is identifying these blind spots.

- Reviewing past decisions and their motivations is an eye-opener. Think back to your choices and ask yourself what drove them. Was it fear, ambition, or perhaps a desire for approval? Understanding these motivations helps you see how they've shaped your life path. It's like opening an unlabeled moving box, ultimately revealing a part of your life.

- Another way to identify blind spots is to get feedback from those around us. It's like asking your friend if your hair looks okay after coming into a building from a windy day. Honest feedback can be a mirror that reveals the things we miss.

- A good source is a 360-degree feedback from colleagues. This includes feedback from managers above you, subordinates below you, peers at your same level, and your "customers" or stakeholders. The feedback form must include questions about your attitude, not just your work. This comprehensive approach gathers insights from everyone you work with, offering a well-rounded view of your behavior.
  Perhaps your team complains that you never get anything approved by your boss that they requested, and you realize it's because you were certain the boss would say "no" so you didn't ask. It's like getting a full-body scan of your professional persona.

- Another method is to think about how you as an objective outsider would answer these feedback questions about yourself. Ask yourself tough questions about how you react in certain situations. Are you the person who volunteers first, then regrets doing so and conveniently forgets to follow up? These questions help illuminate your blind spots, often revealing areas you didn't know needed attention.

- A great technique for revealing bias blind spots is to pay attention to what you criticize about other people in your thoughts. Does that same fault exist in you? We tend to criticize others more for the things of which we're also guilty! Remember, when you point at someone, 3 fingers point back at you.

Leaving these blind spots unaddressed is like ignoring a leaky faucet. The drip-drip-drip seems harmless until the water bill arrives, or worse, the ceiling caves in. Blind spots can impede personal and professional improvement, causing you to miss out on leadership roles requiring strong self-awareness and the ability to interact well with others (called "**emotional intelligence**".) Imagine losing out on a promotion because people perceive you as unapproachable or inflexible, all because of blind spots about which you weren't even aware.

In relationships, these blind spots can lead to ongoing conflicts, where the same issues crop up like weeds in a garden. It's that moment when your partner says, "We've talked about this." You have no recollection of a previous conversation, so you insist, "No, we haven't!" insinuating that they're lying. The truth is that your blind spot kept you from actively listening to the conversation. These recurring issues can erode trust and connection, making it difficult to build lasting, meaningful relationships.

Make It Better

So, what's the game plan for dealing with these blind spots?

- Start by incorporating regular feedback sessions into your personal development plans. Think of it as routine maintenance for your social skills.

- Schedule regular check-ins with trusted colleagues, friends, or family members. Ask for honest thoughts about your behavior and be open to what they say, even if it stings a little. This is your chance to adjust your course before any serious damage is done.

- Additionally, set aside time to think about what you've heard. A quiet moment with your morning coffee can help. Use this time to contemplate recent interactions, considering what went well and what could improve.

- Over time, these strategies can help you avoid the behavioral potholes you had been blind to, paving the way for smoother, more rewarding interactions.

A Pause for Thought

Take the time to identify some of your blind spots.

- What behavior have you exhibited at work that could keep you from getting promoted to a leadership position?

- At home, what behavior does your partner keep getting frustrated about?

5.2 The Personal SWOT Analysis

The **Personal SWOT Analysis**, also called the **Mirror Test**, challenges you to view yourself objectively. It's like looking at a painting up close and then stepping back to see the whole picture. We often get so caught up in the details, such as our daily habits, routines, and quirks, that we forget to see how they all fit together.

This analysis encourages you to step back and examine the bigger picture of your life. Are you living according to your values? Or are you just going through the motions, ticking off tasks on an endless to-do list? Recognizing these discrepancies is like finding that one piece of a puzzle that's been missing all along, suddenly making everything more transparent.

You might be familiar with a SWOT analysis from business settings, but it's surprisingly effective for personal improvement. This tool is about clarity, showing you where you stand and where you could go. It can be goal-focused or a total assessment of yourself.

For personal use, think of the SWOT categories like this.

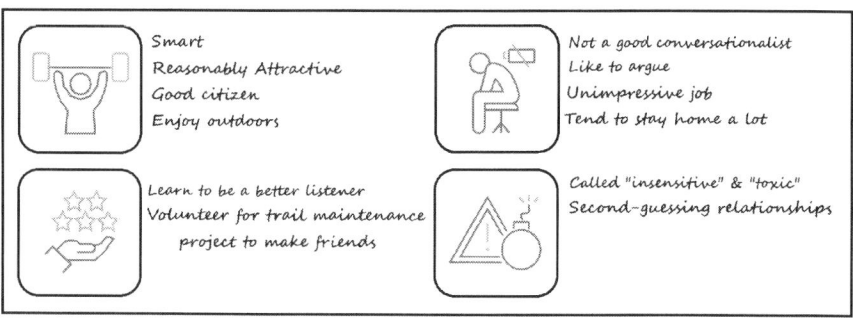

Sample Personal SWOT Analysis

Strengths: These are your superpowers that make you uniquely you.

Weaknesses: This includes your blind spots. You're simply acknowledging areas where you can grow.

Opportunities: These are the chances life throws your way that you might not have considered.

Threats: These are obstacles that seem to crop up just when you're getting ahead.

Make It Better

Applying the insights from a Personal SWOT Analysis is where the magic happens. It's not enough to know your strengths and weaknesses; you need to act on them. Set actionable goals based on what you've discovered.

- If your SWOT analysis revealed a strength in creativity, consider how you can incorporate more creative projects into your life.

- If one of your weaknesses is a lack of organization, don't settle for "I'm not any good at being organized." Consider strategies to improve it.

Developing an action plan to overcome blind spots is vital. The plan should include specific steps to tackle these areas, turning them from weaknesses into opportunities to improve. That improvement could come from continued learning, mentorship, or simply practicing new behaviors. Whatever the path, remember that self-awareness is not a destination but a continuous journey of discovery.

A Pause for Thought

What would your personal SWOT analysis say about you?

- **Strengths**: What are your top three strengths? How do these traits benefit you in your daily life and work?

- **Weaknesses**: What are three areas that you should improve? What steps can you take to address these weaknesses?

- **Opportunities**: What are some opportunities for improvement, advancement, or positive change that you see? How can you capitalize on them?

- **Threats**: What are some potential obstacles or challenges you could have? What strategies can you implement to mitigate these threats?

Think about this framework as a guide for your personal development, revisiting it periodically to adjust for changes.

5.3 Techniques for Looking Inward

Note that this could sound a little like that dreaded touchy-feely stuff, so we're using ordinary language rather than the lingo of pop psychology.

See More Clearly

Looking inward (also called "self-reflection," a trendy buzzword) is like holding a mirror to your soul, giving you a chance to hear from your subconscious. Your subconscious won't talk to your conscious mind when your thoughts are too busy, but it can throw out hints called "intuition" or a "gut feeling."

Write down your thoughts. (This can be called "Journaling," another trendy buzzword.)

- Each day, *after you write your To-Do list to clear your head*, take a moment to jot down any thoughts that pop into your head. It's like conversing with yourself; your pen isn't judging you.

- Maybe you'll write "regret" for that gnawing feeling you haven't been willing to think more about, "excited" for a great idea you want to investigate, or "Mom" for a nudge that you should contact her.

- Writing stuff down helps capture those fleeting thoughts, making them retrievable so you can think about them later.

Think about nothing. (This is called "Meditation.")

- Sit quietly in a relaxing chair. (This reminds me of how my Dad always replied that he wasn't asleep; he was just resting his eyes.)

- As you relax, when busy thoughts intrude, think "away" to push them out and allow the world's chaos to fade into the background.

- This allows your subconscious mind to bubble up to your conscious what it wants to tell you, allowing clarity to emerge. If nothing comes to mind, that's OK.

- If you're religious, this is like prayer, not the part when you ask for stuff, but when you wait for a gut feeling that you discern to be a reply.

- Here's another example of your subconscious communicating with your conscious: You're in the shower, not even thinking about an earlier problem when the solution pops into your head. Eureka!

Ask yourself questions.

- Think about questions like "What could I have done differently?" or "What can I be grateful for today?" This will help you understand these things better.

MAKE IT BETTER

Setting aside time for this "look inward" thinking is important. In today's fast-paced world, carving out a quiet, distraction-free environment can be as hard as finding water in a desert, but it's important.

Establish a consistent routine to make this thinking time more than an afterthought or something you read about in a book. It can be in the morning with your coffee, after exercise, or a quiet moment before bed as you wind down to sleep. This dedicated time allows you to process emotions and experiences, improving your awareness. It's like giving your mind a regular tune-up, ensuring everything runs smoothly.

Look inward for your personal values. By processing your thoughts, you can uncover what really matters to you. It's like finding your internal compass to guide you through life's decisions, big and small.

You might recognize discrepancies between your beliefs and behaviors. For example, you may realize:

- You value honesty but tend to sugarcoat the truth to avoid conflict.
- You only want a loved one to be happy, but you tend to tell them how to live their life based on what might make you happy.

Evaluate past experiences and behaviors, not to dwell but to learn.

- Identify your behavior patterns over time to understand the consequences of past decisions.

- You may notice a tendency to procrastinate, leading to last-minute stress and rushed work.

- You may lash out when things don't go your way, leading to hurt feelings.

- Recognizing these patterns is the first step in changing them. It's like being a detective in your own life, piecing together clues to create a clearer picture of who you are and who you want to become.

This awareness helps you course-correct, ensuring your actions reflect your true self. By understanding what really matters, you can intentionally live as the real "you."

5.4 Emotional Vocabulary Expansion: Name the Unnamable

Imagine trying to describe a rainbow with just two colors. It would be pretty limiting. (I apologize if you're color-blind.) The same goes for our emotions. When our emotional vocabulary is limited, we end up with monochrome words to express a multicolored experience. Having a rich emotional vocabulary helps you precisely identify and express emotions, reducing misunderstandings.

Imagine feeling a tightness in your throat and wanting to scream, "I'm angry!" But wait. Could it be "frustrated" or "disappointed" instead? They're similar but not the same.

Identifying the right emotion helps you address the root cause, such as an annoying colleague or a missed opportunity. Using precise language ensures that you're understood by people, minimizing those frustrating "That's not what I meant" moments.

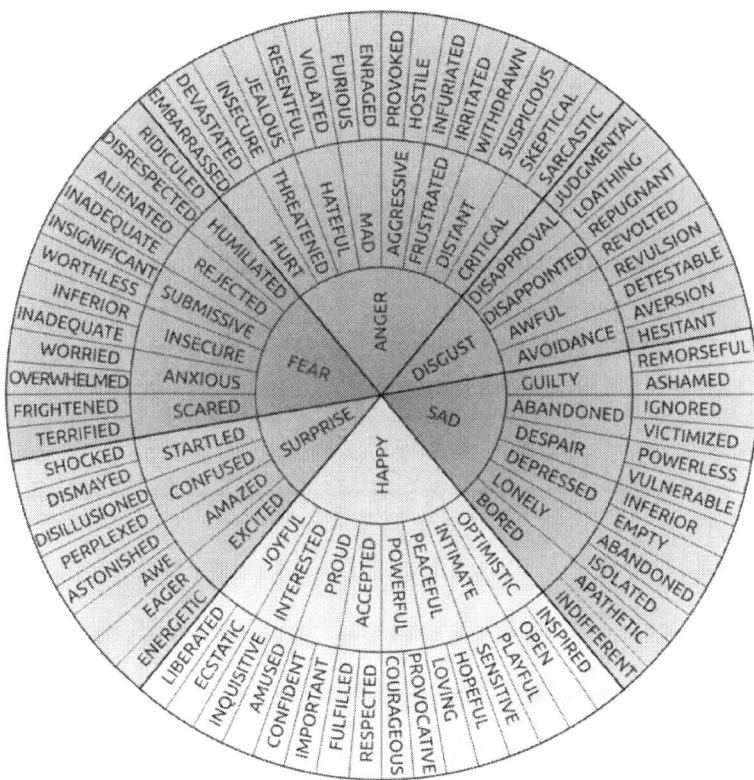

Developing a vocabulary of emotions is about adding more colors to your emotional palette. An emotion wheel chart like the one from Idaho State University can be helpful. It's like a map of the emotional landscape, guiding you to pinpoint exactly where you stand. (Other versions can be found by searching the internet for the words: emotion wheel.)

A Pause for Thought

Review the words on the wheel to enhance your vocabulary and deepen your understanding of the world of emotions.

A well-developed emotional vocabulary can improve communication and build stronger and more intimate relationships. Imagine clearly sharing your feelings, saying, "I'm feeling overwhelmed," instead of the vague "I'm just not happy today." This precision helps people understand your needs and concerns, reducing conflicts.

By using the right words to articulate your precise feelings, you invite people to respond thoughtfully, paving the way for stronger interpersonal connections. It's like handing over a detailed map rather than vague directions, ensuring everyone's on the same page.

5.5 Identify Your Triggers to Manage Them

We've all been there: one minute, you're having a perfect day, and the next, a seemingly innocuous comment sends you spiraling. That's the magic or curse of triggers. They're like emotional tripwires that set off a cascade of reactions, catching us off guard.

See More Clearly

Triggers are specific situations or words that provoke a strong emotional response, often based on past experiences, memories, or deeply personal associations. These triggers can instantly evoke anger, sadness, or joy, impacting your current emotional state.

- Criticism can be one such trigger. A colleague's feedback may feel more like an attack, or a partner's remark about your cooking makes you want to abandon the kitchen forever.

- Rejection is another common culprit. It stings, whether it's a declined invitation or a missed promotion.

- When left unchecked, these triggers can turn small sparks into raging fires, influencing behavior in ways we might not even recognize.

Conflict triggers are like hidden landmines in the landscape of our interactions.

- **Personal insecurities**: This could be a nagging feeling of not being good enough or the fear of being judged. These insecurities can make even the most minor critique feel like an all-out assault on your self-worth.

- **Past unresolved grievances**: Remember that time your best friend forgot to return your call? Yeah, that still stings and, believe it or not, can sneak into present-day arguments.

- **Misunderstandings**: This is when the message delivered isn't quite the message received. It's the email that reads as snippy or the text that lands like a bombshell, even when neither was intended that way.

Make It Better

Identifying your personal triggers requires some detective work. Think of it as piecing together a puzzle, where each piece is a clue to understanding your emotional landscape.

- Start by keeping a trigger list. Jot down moments when you feel an intense emotional reaction. What was said? Who was involved? How did you feel afterward?

- Over time, patterns will emerge, revealing the specific situations that set you off.

- Analyzing past conflicts can also provide insights. Look for common threads in disagreements with partners, friends, or coworkers. There may be a recurring theme, like feeling undervalued or misunderstood, or not being included in decision making.

- These insights are like finding breadcrumbs leading to the heart of your emotional forest.

- Getting feedback from trusted individuals can also illuminate blind spots you might not see. Sometimes, an outside perspective is all it takes to understand why certain situations push your buttons.

Ignoring these triggers is like neglecting a dull toothache; eventually, it gets infected, causing more damage than anticipated. Unrecognized triggers can lead to recurring negative behaviors or escalating conflicts, where the same arguments rear their ugly heads repeatedly.

Have you ever been embroiled in the same argument with your partner, wondering why the issue never seems to get resolved? It's as if you're stuck in a loop, doomed to repeat the same mistakes until you identify the trigger at play. This cycle can erode relationships, leaving both parties frustrated and disconnected. Acknowledging and understanding your triggers opens the door to breaking this cycle.

Managing triggers takes practice and intention. Developing specific coping techniques can help mitigate their impact.

- Taking a deep breath is helpful. When you feel a trigger approaching, pause and take a slow, deep breath. It's like hitting the pause button on your emotions, allowing you to regain control.

- If criticism triggers you, try reminding yourself that it's an opportunity to learn about your blind spot rather than an attack.

- Delaying your response can be beneficial. Instead of reacting immediately, give yourself a moment to think about what's happening. Count to ten, take a walk, or even excuse yourself from the situation. This delay gives you time to think and choose a response rather than acting impulsively.

- Proactive communication is very helpful. Address known triggers before they escalate by discussing them openly with those involved. For example, you might ask your partner to never compare your behavior to your mother's. It's like putting up a "Caution: Wet Floor" sign before someone slips.

- Let people know how specific situations make you feel and collaborate on solutions.

    - Say, for example, "If I'm doing something you don't like, please tell me about that something. Don't mention my mother, regardless of whether she did that same thing." This transparency promotes understanding and cooperation.

    - Try sitting down with your coworker or partner and saying, "Hey, can we talk about this before it becomes a bigger issue?" Acknowledging the emotions involved is necessary to create a space where understanding becomes possible.

- Therapy or counseling can be beneficial for the long-term management of triggers. Exploring these emotional responses with a professional can lead to deeper understanding. (No, the counselor won't conclude that you hate your parents or say you have repressed memories; both are unhelpful myths.) They will help you pick apart your complex web of past experiences that contributed to your current reactions, offering guidance and support as you work through them.

As you become more aware of your triggers and develop ways to manage them, you'll find that they hold less power over your reactions. You'll move from feeling like a puppet on a string to being the one holding the strings, guiding your emotional responses with intention and care.

A Pause for Thought

Identifying Your Triggers

- Think about recent conflicts. What common themes or triggers can you identify?

- How do personal insecurities or past grievances influence your reactions?

- Consider discussing your findings with a trusted friend or partner for additional insights.

5.6 Cognitive Dissonance: Are Feelings of Hypocrisy Making You Toxic?

Imagine cruising a buffet after promising to eat healthfully, only to pile your plate with fried food. Or imagine you're convinced that honesty is the best policy, yet you lie to a friend to avoid an awkward conversation. That uncomfortable feeling that you're a hypocrite is called **cognitive dissonance.**[14].

See More Clearly

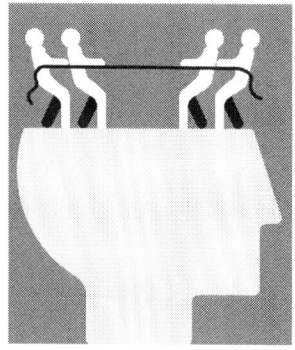

This psychological discomfort arises when your actions clash with your beliefs and intentions. It's like your mind is at war with itself, trying to reconcile two opposing forces.

It's a psychological tug-of-war in which conflicting beliefs or actions create internal tension, nudging you to either justify those behaviors or change them to align with your self-image. It's like trying to fit a square peg into a round hole; something just doesn't sit right, and it gnaws at you until you address it.

This discomfort often drives us to rationalize actions, even when they clash with our values. You might tell yourself that the little lie was necessary or harmless, but deep down, it feels wrong. This internal conflict can fuel toxic responses as we scramble to maintain a façade that everything is fine.

This internal conflict is more common than you might think.

- You value health and sleep yet stay up late and indulge in unhealthy snacks.

- You may value compassion but find yourself snapping at loved ones when stressed.

- You pride yourself on honesty and fairness, but you often cut corners and bend the truth at work, saying what the manager wants to hear.

- You might be a staunch advocate for environmental sustainability but drive a gas-guzzling vehicle because it's so cool.

- Imagine the ethical dilemma at work if you must sell or support a product you don't believe in. The clash between your personal ethics and professional actions can leave you feeling anguished and evasive about telling friends where you work. (I once turned down an opportunity to work for a Payday Lender for this reason.)

These contradictions create tension that nags at you until you address them, like a blister that won't heal. Your hypocritical internal dialogue tries to justify these inconsistencies, telling you it's no big deal, even when it is.

Make It Better

Resolving cognitive dissonance requires mental gymnastics.

- Identifying these sources of internal conflict is the first step toward resolution. Look for places where your actions don't quite match your values. It requires some thinking, like playing detective in your own life.

- These conflicts can arise when new information challenges long-held beliefs. Imagine being a staunch advocate for a particular cause only to discover evidence contradicting your stance. It's a mental wrestling match, forcing you to reevaluate your position or find a way to integrate this new perspective without fracturing your identity.

Take the time to reevaluate and adjust your personal values. Are they really your own, or are they borrowed from someone else's playbook? Sometimes, a shift in perspective can align your beliefs more closely with your actions.

- Discuss your perspective with a trusted friend or mentor. The conversation can challenge your personal narrative, offering perspectives you might not have considered. It's like having a friendly debate where the goal is not to win but to understand.

Gradual behavioral changes can also help. Instead of a drastic overhaul, make small adjustments that lead to a values alignment. It's like learning to ride a bike, wobbly at first but smoother with practice.

> When your actions align with your values, you feel like you're living your truth instead of wearing a mask or playing a role.

Reconciling dissonance has its perks.

- First, there's a boost in self-esteem. You no longer call yourself a hypocrite when your actions align with your values. You feel more genuine, like you're living your truth instead of wearing a mask or playing a role.

- Greater alignment between actions and self-identity results in a sense of peace, where your internal dialogue shifts from justification to acceptance.

- Relationships often improve as well, as loved ones notice that your actions align with your words, and commitments are kept.

5.7 Recap and Check-in

We've examined techniques tailored to people who are skeptical about self-improvement, each offering a unique way to explore your behaviors and reactions. These tools can help you better understand yourself and your impact on those around you.

Identifying your blind spots and analyzing your Strengths, Weaknesses, Opportunities, and Threats can help you begin to see yourself as people see you. We've explored ways to look inward and words to better describe your feelings.

Identifying and managing triggers can improve interactions that once seemed fraught with tension and turn them into opportunities for understanding and connection. We also reviewed how reconciling cognitive dissonance can help align your actions with your values, leading to a more satisfying life.

As we've explored these avenues to look inward, it's important to recognize that this isn't about perfection but progress. These techniques help you make informed choices and take control of your narrative.

> This isn't about perfection; it's about progress.

A Pause for Thought

This chapter aims to provide tools that work with your unique experiences and challenges.

- Finding your blind spots
- A personal SWOT analysis
- Ways to look inward
- Expanding your vocabulary for expressing emotions
- Identifying triggers
- Changing what feels hypocritical

Are there specific techniques that could make a difference in your daily life?

- Take a moment to consider how you might integrate them into your routine, perhaps starting small and building as you go.
- Consider how these techniques can help you navigate the complexities of your relationships at work and home, reducing or eliminating toxic behaviors.

In the next chapter, we'll explore improving communication skills, which are vital to enhancing personal and professional relationships.

See Appendix 1 if you'd like to work through some thought-provoking questions.

Help Us Promote Understanding

"Everything that irritates us about others can lead us to an understanding of ourselves." Carl Jung

Did you know that becoming more aware of yourself can significantly improve your interpersonal relationships and overall satisfaction with life? We believe that promoting understanding is key to personal change, and we're grateful to have you explore this with us.

Here's something to ponder: Would you reconsider a long-held belief if you discovered it could improve your interactions with people, even if it initially made you uncomfortable? Imagine helping someone just like you, skeptical of typical self-help advice but open to genuine, evidence-based insights into changing behaviors.

We aim to challenge misconceptions and promote a more thoughtful approach to stop toxic behavior. We want to reach as many minds as possible and need your candid feedback.

Your voice is powerful. Many people decide which books to read based on recommendations like yours. You're at the halfway point, so I'm asking you to pause and leave a review for ***I'm Not Toxic, You're Overreacting***.

Leaving a review is a straightforward act that takes a moment but can have a significant impact. Your insights can:

- Help one more person recognize and modify unhelpful behaviors.
- Help one more professional enhance their workplace interactions.
- Help one more individual improve their personal relationships.
- Help one more family member understand and address toxic dynamics.
- Help one more story of change begin.

Are you ready to encourage more conversation about toxic behavior? It's simple! Go to this book in your media purchases, and leave your review with a rating, perhaps a video or photo, and your honest thoughts. Links and instructions vary based on which media type you're reading, so details are provided below.

With sincere thanks,
Delia Sikes

To review **the eBook** of *I'm Not Toxic, You're Overreacting*, **please click the appropriate link for your country**. If your country isn't listed, please find the order in your Amazon media purchases.

US: https://www.amazon.com/review/review-your-purchases/?asin=B0F6KTQLDL

Canada: https://www.amazon.ca/review/review-your-purchases/?asin=B0F6KTQLDL

UK: https://www.amazon.co.uk/review/review-your-purchases/?asin=B0F6KTQLDL

Australia: https://www.amazon.com.au/review/review-your-purchases/?asin=B0F6KTQLD

To review **the paperback book** of *I'm Not Toxic, You're Overreacting*, **please scan the appropriate QR code for your country**. If your country isn't listed, please find the order in your Amazon media purchases.

Review Paperback in US

Review Paperback in Canada

Review Paperback in UK

Review Paperback in Australia

To review **the hardcover book** of ***I'm Not Toxic, You're Overreacting*, please scan the appropriate QR code for your country**. If your country isn't listed, please find the order in your Amazon media purchases.

Review Hardcover in US

Review Hardcover in Canada

Review Hardcover in UK

Review Hardcover in Australia

In the Audible app, click the 3 dots by the book in your library listing and select Rate and Review.

Remember that sharing knowledge is one of the best ways to build relationships. If this book has helped you, consider passing it on to someone who might benefit.

To purchase **the paperback book** of ***I'm Not Toxic, You're Overreacting*** for *someone you know who has toxic tendencies*, **please click the appropriate link or scan the QR code for your country**. If your country isn't listed, please search for the title.

HELP US PROMOTE UNDERSTANDING

US: https://www.amazon.com/dp/1967134065

Canada: https://www.amazon.ca/dp/1967134065

UK: https://www.amazon.co.uk/dp/1967134065

Australia: https://www.amazon.com.au/dp/1967134065

Buy Paperback in US

Buy Paperback in Canada

Buy Paperback in UK

Buy Paperback in Australia

CHAPTER 6

IMPROVE COMMUNICATION SKILLS

You're at a backyard barbecue, the sun is shining, burgers are sizzling, and your friend is recounting an epic tale of their latest adventure. But instead of hanging onto every word, you find yourself nodding along while mentally trying to solve a problem at work. We've all been there, lost in thought while someone is speaking.

6.1 Listening vs. Hearing

It's the classic case of hearing versus listening.

- **Hearing** functions like the background music at the grocery store; it's there, but you're not tuned in.

- On the other hand, **listening** is like tuning into your favorite podcast, where every word matters. It's intentional, active, and requires your full attention.

According to Very Well Mind article, "What's The Difference Between Hearing and Listening?", hearing is a passive process, while listening is an active one that involves effort and focus[15].

See More Clearly

This distinction between hearing and listening is more than just semantics.

- When you only hear someone, you're likely to miss the nuances of their message, leading to misunderstandings and misinterpretations. Imagine being in a meeting where you're nodding but not absorbing what's being said. It's like watching a movie with the sound off; you get the gist, but you're missing the plot.

- In contrast, really listening (called "active listening") can improve these interactions. It's about engaging with the speaker, processing the information, and responding thoughtfully. When you really listen, you show the speaker that you value their words and insights. They, in turn, feel heard and understood.

Make It Better

Focus on these two behaviors to improve your listening skills.

1. **Eliminate distractions** during conversations. Put down your phone, close that extra browser tab, and give the person in front of you your

full attention. It's like putting a "Do Not Disturb" sign in front of other thoughts, allowing you to focus entirely on the interaction.

2. **Paraphrase and summarize** what you heard. After someone speaks, verify what you think you heard. This shows that you're engaged and helps clarify any misunderstandings. It doesn't have to mean you agree with them.

This can sometimes feel awkward if you're merely following a script. To make repeating what you've heard feel more natural and less like a mechanical process, consider these strategies:

- **Paraphrase thoughtfully**: Instead of repeating the speaker's words verbatim, rephrase their message in your own words. For instance, if someone says, "I've been overwhelmed at work, and it's stressing me out," you might respond with a question tone of voice, "So your job has been really demanding lately, and it's getting to you?"

- **Summarize the main points**: Briefly summarize the speaker's key points to demonstrate understanding. This can be particularly effective in longer conversations or meetings. For example, "So, to make sure I understand, you're concerned about the upcoming project deadlines and the current team dynamics?"

- **Recognize and state their feelings**: Sometimes, the emotions behind the words are more important than the words. Repeating back their feelings can help the speaker feel understood on a deeper level. If someone describes a situation that sounds frustrating, you might say, "It sounds like you're really frustrated by how things are going."

- **Ask clarifying questions**: If repeating back what was said feels awkward, pivot slightly and ask questions to clarify your understanding. This keeps the conversation flowing and shows genuine interest. For example, "When you mention feeling overlooked, are you referring to when we recognized Mike and Tom's success in last week's meeting or something else?" Continue with open-ended questions (those that can't be answered with a "yes" or "no.")

- **Use nonverbal cues**: Nodding, maintaining eye contact, and using appropriate facial expressions can communicate that you are listening and understanding without interrupting or repeating everything.

- **Incorporate what they said into your response**: Use what you've heard as a foundation for your response, which can make the conversation feel more organic. For instance, "I get that you're upset about the decision. What do you think would be the best next step?"

Poor listening can perpetuate toxic interactions. When you fail to listen, you risk jumping to conclusions or misinterpreting the speaker's intent, which can fuel conflicts.

Imagine a colleague giving you feedback, but you're too busy planning your rebuttal to hear their concern. You miss the reason for the conversation plus an opportunity for improvement, and the conversation descends into talking "at" one another instead of with each other.

Conversely, actively listening opens the door to meaningful dialogue, reducing the chances of conflict and building a collaborative environment where everyone contributes.

> Put down your phone, close that extra browser tab, and give the person in front of you your full attention.

A Pause for Thought

The next time you're in a conversation, try these steps:

- Focus on listening actively.

- After the person speaks, verify what they said using your own words.

- Ask open-ended questions to go deeper, pursuing your curiosity.

- Notice the difference this makes in the quality of your interactions and the connections you build.

6.2 Assertive vs. Aggressive: Find the Right Balance

Have you ever noticed how some people seem to have a knack for getting their point across without ruffling feathers while others leave a trail of chaos in their wake? That's the difference between assertive and aggressive communication.

- Assertiveness is the middle path, steering clear of both passivity and aggression. It empowers you to express your needs and desires respectfully and clearly, opening the door to constructive dialogue and stronger relationships. It's like the Goldilocks of communication styles: not too hot or cold, just right.

- It isn't just about your tone of voice. It's about expressing your needs clearly and respectfully without bulldozing over people. For example, you could say, "I feel overwhelmed with this project timeline and need some adjustments," instead of barking, "This @#&?%!! deadline is insane and needs to change now!"

- Assertiveness respects the other person's perspective, creating a dialogue rather than a monologue. It's about maintaining mutual respect, not disregarding others to get your way.

Make It Better

So, how do you nail assertiveness without slipping into aggression?

- One powerful technique is using "I" statements. Instead of saying, "You interrupted me," try, "I feel unheard when I'm interrupted." It shifts the focus from blame to personal feelings, paving the way for constructive dialogue.

- Setting clear boundaries is another key strategy. It's like having a fence around your garden, clearly marking what's okay and what's not. By stating your expectations upfront, you prevent misunderstandings and create a foundation for healthy interactions. For example, tell your coworker, "I need an uninterrupted period from 2-3 PM to focus on this report," rather than respond angrily to an interruption.

Assertiveness promotes mutual respect and understanding. It's like laying down a welcome mat that says, "Your thoughts matter, and so do mine." This approach enhances decision-making by encouraging open and honest communication. Everyone gets a seat at the table, and different perspectives are considered, leading to more balanced and well-informed decisions. It's the key to a collaborative environment where everyone contributes and feels valued.

Try turning aggressive reactions into assertive responses with a friend who's willing to give you feedback. It's about keeping things in perspective so you're not loud and argumentative when voicing your needs. With practice, assertiveness becomes second nature, improving your relationships.

> Assertiveness is about keeping things in perspective so you're not loud and argumentative when voicing your needs.

6.3 Feedback: Giving and Receiving without Defensiveness

"Feedback" is that word that can make your shoulders slump with dread and your heart race like you drank a double espresso. We're told it's important and know it can be productive, yet it feels like navigating a minefield of criticism.

Feedback can be a helpful tool for personal and professional learning. It illuminates areas for improvement, helping you identify blind spots, improving your skills. It's like a GPS for your personal development journey, rerouting you to a smoother road.

Giving and receiving feedback isn't just about pointing out what's wrong. It's also about reinforcing positive behaviors, letting you know when you're on the right track. Imagine a coach cheering you on during a marathon, offering encouragement and guidance.

Giving Feedback

When giving feedback, the goal is to be helpful, not harmful.

- Start by using specific examples to support your observations. Instead of saying, "You're always late," try, "I noticed you arrived after the meeting started a couple of times last week." It's like providing evidence rather than vague opinions.

- Focus on behavior rather than personal attributes. Critiquing someone's actions rather than their character keeps the conversation constructive. It's the difference between saying, "This report needs more detail," versus, "You did a lousy job on this report." One targets the work's shortcomings, and the other targets the person's initiative. The former invites improvement, and the latter invites defensiveness.

Receiving Feedback

Receiving feedback can feel like standing under a spotlight, every flaw magnified. (Oh, how I hate it!)

Try to maintain an open and receptive mindset.

- **Separate Yourself from the Feedback**: Try to view the feedback as being about specific behaviors or actions, not about you as a person. This can reduce feeling attacked and make feedback more manageable.

- **Listen Fully Before Responding**: Listen to the entire feedback without interrupting. Often, feedback includes criticisms, suggestions and insights that can be valuable once any emotional response has subsided.

- **Pause Before Reacting**: Take a deep breath and give yourself a moment to process the feedback. You want to manage initial emotional reactions and prepare a more thoughtful response.

- **Get Clarification**: Ask clarifying questions if you have questions or doubts about the criticism. This engages the giver in a dialogue, which can soften the perceived negativity.

- **Ask for Specific Examples**: If the feedback is vague, ask for specific examples to better understand the issue. This can shift the focus from emotions to facts.

- **Express Appreciation**: Even if the feedback is hard to hear, thank the person for their input. Acknowledging their effort to help you improve can make the conversation more constructive.

- **Think About the Feedback**: Take some time to think about the feedback privately. Consider whether it contains truths and how you can use it to improve. Separating yourself from the person who delivered the feedback can provide a clearer perspective.

- **Develop an Action Plan**: Identify steps you can take to address the feedback. You may disagree with the criticism and need to fix what makes people perceive you that way. This proactive approach can help shift your focus from feeling criticized to taking control.

- **Discuss Your Feelings**: If feedback feels harsh or harms your self-esteem, try discussing your feelings with a mentor, friend, coach, or therapist. Their third-party perspective on the feedback and your reactions to it can be enlightening.

- **Be Kind to Yourself**: Everyone receives criticism at some point; it's a part of learning and growing. It doesn't diminish your value or capabilities.

If you struggle to be receptive, adopt a detached mindset so you can maintain composure and think later about the feedback you've received.

- **Play the Role of Advocate**: Think of the person being evaluated as another person not in the room, and you are the problem solver who will make notes of the feedback and help that person improve. Then, state that you will respond to the reviewer later.

- **Separate Your Inner and Outer Self**: Remember that they're offering feedback for the "outer" version of you as you come across, not the "inner" version of who you are or want to be. The feedback can enlighten the "inner" you on ways that the "outer" you isn't coming across as who you want to be.

- **Maybe It Wasn't a Priority**: Feedback is like being handed the right puzzle piece that helps fill in the picture. Instead of jumping to defend your puzzle as not missing a piece or not having a wrong piece, pause to consider whether you missed examining that part of the puzzle closely because it wasn't a priority. Consider how the reviewer's insight might bring that part of the puzzle to your attention and help improve it. (I defended myself by saying that the business of serving the end customer was my priority, not the busyness of other tasks.)

These approaches can suppress tension and allow productive dialogue. It's not a battle to be won.

Creating a culture of feedback within teams can change feedback from a dreaded chore into a helpful tool for your ongoing development.

6.4 Non-verbal Cues: The Unspoken Language of Interaction

Have you ever tried conversing with someone who keeps their arms crossed, their eyes darting around the room, or staring at a computer, barely glancing at you? It's like they are present but not participating. Have you been that person? I'm sure I have.

Nonverbal cues (also called body language) are subtle signals we send with our facial expressions, gestures, posture, and even tone of voice. They're like the subtitles to our spoken words, sometimes revealing more truth about our attitude than we intend.

- When you lean in during a conversation, it shows engagement and interest.

- On the flip side, crossed arms can say a person is not receptive to what they're hearing, all without a single word being spoken.

- Eye contact, or the lack of it, can convey everything from confidence to discomfort.

- It's like playing charades, except your body is doing the talking.

Understanding non-verbal cues can be a game-changer in successfully relating to people. For instance, a smile often invites warmth and openness, while a frown or sneer might signal disapproval or annoyance.

Recognizing these signals helps you read the room better and adjust your approach accordingly. If someone's leaning in, it's a cue they're interested in what you're saying, inviting you to dive deeper into the conversation. But if they're tapping their foot or repeatedly checking the time of day, you should wrap things up. Reading this body language lets you tune into the unspoken undercurrents of communication.

Non-verbal cues don't stand alone; they complement and sometimes contradict what's being said. Imagine someone saying, "I'm fine," with squinting eyes, a clenched jaw and tense shoulders. The words say one thing, but the body tells a different story.

When verbal and non-verbal cues align, they reinforce each other, creating a clear and consistent message. But when they don't, it leads to mixed signals, leaving the listener doubting what was said. It's like watching a movie where the subtitles don't match the dialogue. Avoid this by making sure your body language matches your words. This will authenticate your interactions.

MAKE IT BETTER

Improving your non-verbal communication skills starts with awareness.

- Begin by analyzing the body language of those around you. Notice how people's gestures and expressions change in different situations. It's like studying a new language, where practice makes perfect.

- Take a moment to consider your own nonverbal signals. Are your arms always crossed when you're talking? Do you make eye contact or look elsewhere? Correcting these things can soften any perceptions of toxic behavior.

6.5 Overcome the Echo Chamber

Imagine a room where everyone nods in agreement, smiles are exchanged, and viewpoints are mirrored. It's **the echo chamber effect**, also called "being surrounded by yes-men" or "rubber stamping," where voices bounce around without getting challenged. It's like being in a room full of mirrors reflecting your thoughts back at you, reinforcing your beliefs without question.

While it feels nice to have everyone agree with you, it might be artificial agreement if you tend to blurt out toxic responses to contrary thoughts. It limits open dialogue and keeps you stuck in a naïve bubble. This lack of variety means reduced exposure to new ideas, stifling creativity and innovation.

Diverse perspectives are advantageous because they can challenge us and push the boundaries of our thinking. Getting different viewpoints encourages critical thinking and innovation. It's like adding spices to a bland dish, making it more flavorful.

Make It Better

Breaking out of the echo chamber requires intention, curiosity, and the willingness to possibly be wrong.

- Start by having conversations with people with contrasting viewpoints rather than expecting agreement. Admitting you don't have all the answers might feel uncomfortable, but it's necessary for learning.

- Attend events where varied opinions are welcomed. Anticipate listening, talking, and learning rather than debating.

- Explore media and literature that challenge your current beliefs.

It's like opening a window in a stuffy room, letting fresh air and new ideas flow in. These interactions enrich your understanding, adding layers of depth to your worldview.

With a broader view, you become more adaptable and can easily navigate change. Welcoming perspectives different from your own enhances your communication and deepens your relationships, creating more meaningful connections.

6.6 Recap and Check-in

We've explored how communication can either build bridges or erect barriers. We reviewed how to actively listen, from removing distractions to paraphrasing what you heard.

As we contrasted assertive and aggressive communication, we illuminated the effectiveness of expressing needs without turning into a bulldozer. It's about mutual respect, where your voice is heard without drowning out others.

Feedback offers navigation for personal and professional development. By integrating regular feedback into your goals, you invite new opportunities. Creating a culture of feedback builds an environment of collaboration.

The silent language of nonverbal cues, like expressions, gestures, and tone of voice, aids understanding when in agreement with your words. Paying attention to nonverbal signals can change misunderstandings into meaningful interactions.

Finally, breaking free from the confirming echo chamber of continuous agreement broadens your horizons, inviting diverse perspectives that enrich your understanding.

A Pause for Thought

Consider how these skills play out in your everyday life.

- Are you the type who nods along in conversations, or are you engaged and ready to paraphrase and clarify to ensure understanding?

- Have you tried using "I" statements to express your feelings? Have you learned to proactively set boundaries so people can respect your feelings?

- Are you aware of your body language and how it affects your communication?

- Have you ventured beyond your comfort zone, having conversations that challenge your beliefs?

- Will you challenge yourself to engage with those around you in ways that build connection rather than division?

In the next chapter, we'll talk about managing conflict constructively and turning potential disputes into opportunities for understanding and collaboration.

See Appendix 1 if you'd like to work through some thought-provoking questions.

CHAPTER 7

MANAGE CONFLICT CONSTRUCTIVELY

You're arguing with your partner about something as trivial as who left the milk out. Suddenly, you're not arguing about dairy anymore; you're dragging out every unresolved grievance since the dawn of time. Does that sound familiar? It's like opening Pandora's box, where every past slight and insecurity rushes out to join the chaos. Welcome to the world of escalating conflict, where ordinary disagreements get provoked into epic showdowns.

7.1 Strategies for De-escalation: Keep Cool in Heated Moments

In a heated argument, your heart races and you can end up very close to saying something you'll regret. We've all been there. The trick to keeping calm is to hit the brakes before the situation spirals out of control.

- Start by taking a slow, deep breath to reset your emotional state and tell your brain to chill out.

- Counting to ten and taking a deep breath slows your heart rate and gives you a moment to think before you speak.

- If you're still feeling the heat, sometimes a strategic timeout is the best course of action. Stepping away for a few minutes can make the difference between escalating and cooling a conflict. It's not about avoiding the issue but allowing everyone to regroup and approach the conversation with a clear head.

See More Clearly

De-escalation can create a space where rational discussion takes center stage.

- Lowering the emotional temperature makes way for more productive conflict resolution.

- When tensions drop, both parties are more likely to listen and be heard, paving the way for understanding rather than further discord.

- It's like turning down the volume on a blaring radio; suddenly, you can hear the melody beneath the noise.

- In this calmer environment, solutions become more apparent, and finding common ground isn't as daunting as it seemed minutes ago.

MAKE IT BETTER

Words have power, especially when tempers are flaring. Using language that de-escalates tension can make a huge difference.

- Try saying, "Let's take a step back and revisit this calmly." It shows a willingness to pause and think, signaling that you're not interested in a shouting match.

- Or use, "I understand your perspective and want to find a solution." This phrase validates the other person's feelings, making them more receptive to dialogue. It's like pouring water on a smoldering fire, easing the intensity and allowing cooler heads to prevail.

Really listening plays a pivotal role in de-escalation.

- When you actively listen, you show that their viewpoint matters.

- Repeating what you heard in your own words ensures understanding and prevents misinterpretation, which often fuels conflict. Consider saying, "So what I hear you saying is..." This simple repetition can confirm understanding and demonstrate compassion.

- It's not just about hearing words; it's about understanding the emotions behind them. Making this connection creates an environment where conflict can turn into a constructive conversation.

7.2 IDENTIFYING THE REAL ISSUES BEHIND SURFACE CONFLICTS

Understanding the underlying causes of conflict requires searching for the root cause.

- In the workplace, disagreements stem from emotional triggers such as feeling undervalued or overlooked. If your colleague seems unusually defensive during meetings, it might be less about the content of the conversation and more about their past experiences of being sidelined.

- Historical grievances can also play a significant role in family arguments, where a seemingly trivial remark can reopen old wounds. Perhaps that remark about the burnt toast touched a long-standing feeling of being unappreciated. By digging deeper, you can uncover the emotional layers that often drive these conflicts.

MAKE IT BETTER

Dig to unearth root causes.

- One effective technique is asking probing questions that peel back the layers of the issue. Instead of focusing on the immediate disagreement, inquire about the motivations behind it. "What's really bothering you about this task?" can open the door to a more meaningful conversation.

- Really listening is equally crucial in this detective work. By actively listening to what the other person is saying, you can uncover hidden concerns that might otherwise remain buried. It's about paying attention not just to the words but to the emotions and intentions behind them, so people feel safe expressing their feelings.

- A desire to be the leader can be a root cause. In collaborative projects, team members can wrestle for control, and these struggles can lead to recurring conflicts if left unchecked.

- Unspoken expectations can create a recurring storm of conflicts in personal relationships. It's like two ships passing in the night, each heading in the wrong direction because they're too busy avoiding the iceberg to use the lighthouse of communication. By identifying the patterns of conflicts over unspoken expectations, you can address the expectations as the root cause.

Differentiating between symptoms and causes is crucial in resolving conflicts effectively.

1. Consider the frequent arguments about chores, a classic surface symptom. Beneath this lies the deeper cause, such as resentment over perceived inequality in household responsibilities. It's like suppressing

a cough without resting to get over the cold; you might alleviate the symptom temporarily, but the root issue remains.

2. By identifying the deeper causes, you can address the core of the problem, resulting in a more harmonious environment. It's about moving beyond the immediate conflict to understand what's driving it, allowing you to resolve disputes with insight.

A Pause for Thought

Set aside time to think about a recent conflict. Ask yourself:

- What were the surface symptoms?
- What might have been the underlying causes?
- Try to gain insight into the dynamics at play and how addressing root causes could lead to more effective resolution in the future.

Understanding the underlying causes of conflict allows you to navigate disputes with greater awareness and understanding.

7.3 The Role of Compromise

Compromise is like the duct tape of relationships: it's not always pretty, but it does hold things together. At its core, compromise is about balancing competing interests and finding that elusive middle ground in disagreements. It's the art of give-and-take, where both parties make concessions to reach a mutually acceptable solution.

> Compromise is the duct tape of relationships.
> It's like saying,
> "I value our relationship more than being right."

Imagine two people pulling on opposite ends of a tug-of-war rope. Compromise is the moment they decide to stop pulling and instead both give a little to ensure neither ends up in the mud puddle that represents losing. It's not about winning or losing but about ensuring that both sides feel heard and valued.

Compromise has both benefits and challenges.

- On the plus side, compromise helps preserve relationships through mutual concessions, showing that you're willing to bend a little for the sake of harmony. It's like saying, "I value our relationship more than being right."

- However, there's a fine line between healthy compromise and giving up too much, leading to dissatisfaction. If one person continually sacrifices their needs, resentment can brew.

- Finding a balance is crucial, ensuring neither party feels shortchanged in the process.

MAKE IT BETTER

For compromise to be effective, a few techniques can ensure fairness and satisfaction.

- First, set clear boundaries and priorities. Know what you're willing to compromise on and what remains non-negotiable. It's like drawing a map before heading on a road trip, ensuring you don't venture too far off course and arrive late.

- Engage in collaborative decision-making, where both parties actively participate in finding a solution. This approach promotes a sense of ownership and investment in the outcome. When everyone has a say, the resolution becomes a shared victory, strengthening the bond between the individuals involved.

Let's look at compromises in action.

- Imagine a couple facing a budgetary disagreement. One partner wants a vacation, while the other insists on saving for future expenses. By prioritizing essential needs and finding a way to allocate funds for both savings and a modest trip, they reach a decision that respects both perspectives.

- Consider a scheduling conflict at work where two team members need the same day off, leaving a lack of coverage. Through open dialogue and shared flexibility, they agree to alternate days, ensuring both can enjoy their time without disrupting work responsibilities.

These scenarios highlight how compromise can resolve conflicts by navigating disagreements with grace and understanding.

7.4 Collaborative Problem Solving: A Win-Win Approach

Imagine that you're trying to decide on the perfect vacation spot during a family dinner. One person wants the mountains, another the beach, and someone else is suggesting a staycation in the backyard. It's a classic case of conflicting interests but a perfect scenario for **collaborative problem-solving**.

This approach is all about joint ownership of both the problem and the solution, where every voice is heard, and the outcome represents a collective effort. By bringing each person's perspective to the table, you enhance creativity and innovation because two (or more) heads are better than one. When everyone feels invested, the solutions are richer and more satisfying.

See More Clearly

Collaborative problem-solving isn't just a strategy, it's a **perspective** that changes conflicts into opportunities for cooperation and learning.

So, how do you go about it?

- Start by identifying shared goals and interests. What does everyone have in common? For example, maybe everyone agrees that the vacation should be relaxing.

- Next, generate multiple options before settling on one. Brainstorming is your best technique. Throw out every idea, no matter how wild, and see what sticks. However, don't criticize suggestions, or they can stop coming.

- Once you have a list, evaluate each option based on mutual benefit. What gives the greatest number of people what they want? It's like piecing together a puzzle where every piece matters.

- In our opening scenario, by listening to everyone's preferences, they might decide on a cabin near a lake, offering both mountain hikes and beach-like relaxation. Such scenarios highlight how collaboration leads to solutions that satisfy all interests while strengthening relationships.

- This structured approach ensures that the solution isn't just a compromise but a win-win for everyone involved.

By focusing on collaboration rather than competition, you build trust and lay the foundation for future interactions.

Consider a team project at work that brought together individuals from different departments.

- Everyone wanted the project to succeed. The team members used this common goal as a springboard for discussion.

- They employed principled negotiation, which emphasizes interests over positions.

- Each member contributed a unique perspective, and the team explored the underlying motivations behind each party's needs.

- The team's collaboration led to innovative results that no single person could have achieved alone.

Make It Better

To make collaborative problem-solving even smoother, incorporate practical tools.

- Organize brainstorming sessions with clear guidelines to keep ideas flowing without judgment.

- Use decision-making frameworks, like pros and cons lists, to weigh each option's merits and drawbacks.

- These tools act as a roadmap, guiding the group through the twists and turns of negotiation and decision-making. Everyone feels safe expressing their thoughts, knowing that their input is integral to finding the best solution.

Of course, collaboration isn't always smooth sailing. Dominant personalities can overshadow quieter team members, stifling the flow of ideas. To manage this, create space for everyone to contribute by actively inviting input from all team members. It's like hosting a dinner party where everyone is invited by the host to share their story. Encourage quieter voices to speak up, ensuring that no one is left out. (I did this when I was foreman of a jury to ensure fair deliberation.)

Overcoming resistance to change and new ideas can also be a hurdle. Some team members may cling to the status quo, fearing the unknown. Address these concerns by highlighting the benefits of innovation and reassuring them of their value in the process.

Collaborative problem-solving is more than finding solutions; it's about building a team that thrives on trust, creativity, and cooperation. When teams work together, they achieve more than any individual could alone, paving the way for success and fulfillment.

7.5 Set Boundaries for Healthy Relationships

If you picture a garden without fences or borders, it can be hard to tell where the flowers end and the neighbor's weeds begin. Boundaries are like garden fences, crucial for maintaining separation and healthy relationships. They protect your values and needs, ensuring you don't get tangled in others' expectations.

By setting clear boundaries, you can prevent resentment from taking root like weeds in your personal space.

- Without boundaries, over-reach by other people means that burnout is inevitable. You give, give, and give, until there's nothing left but a shell of your former self.

- When you know your limits, you can take care of your own well-being while still being present for other people.

Make It Better

Effectively communicating boundaries starts with assertive communication. It's about expressing your limits clearly and respectfully, like saying, "I love you, but I need my space right now."

Consistency is key. Enforcing boundaries one day and letting them slide the next is like having a fence with missing planks. Mixed signals confuse those around you, leading to boundary breaches. Being consistent helps people understand your needs and ensures your boundaries are respected, whether at work or at home.

Setting and maintaining boundaries comes with its own set of challenges.

- Fear of confrontation or rejection often holds people back, making them hesitate to speak up. It's like walking on eggshells, afraid that asserting your needs will lead to conflict. But remember, boundaries aren't walls but guidelines for healthier interactions.

- Negotiating boundaries with those who resist can be tricky, requiring patience and persistence. Some might push back, testing your resolve.

Stay calm and firm, reinforcing the importance of your needs while remaining open to compromise.

When boundaries are clear, relationships thrive.

- They promote mutual respect and understanding, as both parties know what to expect. Trust blossoms like flowers in a well-tended garden.

- Communication improves, with each person feeling secure and autonomous.

- It's a win-win scenario where you're free to be yourself without fear of overstepping or being overwhelmed.

Boundaries allow you to engage with people on your terms, creating a balanced dynamic where everyone feels valued and heard. They are the foundation of healthy, lasting connections, and they can include saying no to extra work or creating personal time in a busy schedule.

7.6 Turn Disagreements into Opportunities

Conflict is an uninvited guest who shows up at the worst possible moments, stirring up trouble and discomfort. But what if we viewed conflict not as an adversary but as a teacher? Reinterpreting conflicts as opportunities to learn can improve how we handle disputes.

Each conflict is like a mirror, reflecting **personal triggers** and **biases** that might otherwise go unnoticed. This helps you gain insights into your behavioral patterns and offers a chance to develop stronger communication skills.

Resolving conflicts strengthens relationships, turning tension into trust. Imagine the bonds forged by weathering a storm together, emerging on the other side with a deeper understanding and respect for each other.

Make It Better

So, how do you use disagreements as a springboard for learning?

- Start by thinking about the lessons hidden within every conflict. Each disagreement carries a piece of wisdom waiting to be uncovered. Ask yourself what you can learn from this experience. It could be about patience, or it could be about standing your ground.

- Make use of what you learned. It's like using conflict as a mirror to reflect areas where you can improve. These lessons learned are training to help you become a better version of yourself.

- Welcome the idea that every conflict is a learning opportunity, not just a hurdle to overcome.

> **Every conflict is a learning opportunity, not just a hurdle to overcome.**

Real-life examples demonstrate how conflicts can lead to positive change.

- Consider a workplace dispute over project roles that, once addressed, led to improved processes and team dynamics. By tackling the issue head-on, the team discovered more efficient ways to collaborate, increasing productivity and morale.

- On a personal level, think of a family argument about holiday plans that eventually built deeper connections. The disagreement prompted an open conversation about everyone's needs and preferences, resulting in a plan that satisfied all. These scenarios show that when navigated thoughtfully, conflicts can yield benefits far beyond the initial tension.

Open-mindedness is your best ally in changing conflict into learning.

- Welcome feedback and differing opinions as catalysts for change. It's like adding seasoning to a dish, enhancing the flavor and richness of your experiences. A "continuous learning" frame of mind ensures you're always open to new information and ready to adapt and evolve.

- This openness changes conflict from a stumbling block into a steppingstone toward a more harmonious life. When you approach disagreements with curiosity and a willingness to learn, you turn challenges into opportunities for better connection.

A Pause for Thought

Think back to a dispute that escalated quickly. What strategies did you use to resolve it? Did you find success by staying calm and listening, or did you meet frustration with force?

Recognizing these strategies helps you identify what works and what doesn't. It's also important to acknowledge areas for improvement. Maybe you realize that your tone could have been softer or that you could have shown more understanding. This is not about criticism; it's about learning and evolving, like a craftsman refining their skills over time.

When you successfully navigate a conflict, take a moment to acknowledge it as a moment of learning successfully implemented. With each resolved conflict, you become better equipped to handle whatever life throws your way.

7.7 Recap and Check-in

Let's consider the strategies we've explored to manage conflict constructively. You might wonder if these techniques can truly make a difference in your life. Imagine a world where conflicts don't leave you feeling agitated or defeated but instead offer a chance for understanding and learning.

Consider the concept of de-escalation as a tool to transform heated moments into opportunities for clarity and connection. By staying calm and using language that soothes rather than inflames, you can create an environment where solutions can thrive.

We reviewed the importance of finding the root cause for surface-level conflicts to resolve them and how compromise can bridge the gap between opposing views when getting along is more important than the dispute. We talked about the Win-Win results of collaboration. By adopting a collaborative mindset, you're not just solving problems but building relationships grounded in mutual respect. It's about recognizing that when handled thoughtfully, disagreements can strengthen bonds rather than break them.

We explored the importance of setting boundaries to protect your well-being. Let's not forget the potential of turning disagreements into learning opportunities. Each conflict holds a lesson, a chance to see things from a different angle and learn from the experience.

Whether dealing with a difficult colleague at work or navigating family dynamics at home, these strategies offer a path to more harmonious interactions.

In the next chapter, we'll explore the concepts behind empathy and emotional intelligence and how they apply directly to real life, regardless of the buzzwords.

See Appendix 1 if you'd like to work through some thought-provoking questions.

CHAPTER 8

EI AND EMPATHY: REALITY BEHIND THE BUZZWORDS

You're in a meeting, and the tension in the room is obvious. It's like everyone's holding their breath, waiting for someone to throw out an idea to get shredded, a sacrificial lamb. Then, someone speaks up, offering a thoughtful solution, and suddenly, the room's balloon of tension deflates with relief.

CAPABILITIES

Do you know what **"Emotional intelligence" (EI)** is? It enables these capabilities:

1. The ability to **read the room**,

2. **Understand the emotions** swirling around, and

3. Respond in a way that **brings people together** rather than pushing them apart.

Think about it. These skills have always been important, but it took until the early 1990s for them to be named. [16]

8.1 BUILD SOCIAL SKILLS TO BANISH TOXIC BEHAVIORS

LEARN 4 SKILLS FOR EI

EI capabilities are developed from these **4 skills: self-awareness, self-regulation, social awareness, and relationship management**. It's about knowing your own emotional landscape and navigating the emotions of other people with empathy and skill.

Self-awareness is understanding yourself. It's like having a mirror that reflects your outer appearance and inner workings. When you're aware of yourself, you recognize your feelings and how they affect your thoughts and actions.

Self-regulation follows, helping you manage your emotions. It keeps you from sending that angry email or snapping at your partner over something trivial. Relaxing and taking time to think about things can improve your emotional management and help you stay calm, even when emotions run high.

Social awareness means tuning into the emotional currents of those around you, and **relationship management** involves using that awareness to promote positive interactions. Together, they help you build stronger connections in both personal and professional settings.

More Capabilities

Having a high EI gives you even more capabilities.

- **Conflict Resolution**: Instead of letting disagreements fester, you can address issues head-on with understanding and tact. This skill is invaluable whether you're mediating between feuding coworkers or smoothing over a spat at home.

- **Empathy**: You can step into other people's shoes and truly grasp their perspectives. It's not just nodding along; it's really connecting and understanding their experiences. It doesn't require that you agree with them and support their perspective; you simply understand it.

- As discussed earlier in the book, **active listening** isn't just about hearing words; it's about really listening and being fully engaged.

- **Resilience**: Life throws curveballs, but with high EI, you bounce back from adversity like a pro, adapting to challenges.

Risks

EI's hidden hazard is **Emotional Biases**, a type of cognitive bias in which emotions influence reasoning and decisions *without awareness*. These biases come from personal feelings, moods, or a desire for a specific outcome. Even a person with strong EI skills can be tripped up by emotional biases.

These biases can cloud judgment, leading to skewed decisions.

- A recruiter might favor a particular candidate for hire because of their similarity to a favorite relative.

- An investor might keep a poorly performing stock due to a feeling of optimism without merit.

The trick is to recognize these biases and question them.

- Why do you feel like making a decision that is not logical?

- Is it based on past experiences or assumptions?

- A friend or colleague can provide an outside perspective on your emotional interactions.

8.2 Practical Steps to Understand People

You're at a coffee shop with a friend who's clearly overwhelmed with work. They finally open up, venting about the stress that's been mounting. Instead of just nodding along like a bobblehead, you know how to express empathy. You lean in and say, "Wow, I understand how you must feel. That sounds really challenging." This simple act of confirming their emotions is like offering a soft pillow when someone needs it most. When you add, "I'm here; how can I help?" it reinforces that you're not just listening but ready to support them through their turmoil. These responses are about creating a space where people feel safe to express themselves.

Empathy isn't just about feeling sorry for someone or nodding while they talk. It's about truly understanding and sharing what other people feel. Your friend tells you about a rough day, and instead of offering a generic "that's too bad," you really tune in. You ask questions, listen without interrupting, and genuinely care about their experience.

When people connect with mutual respect, that's empathy. The connection turns acquaintances into friends and colleagues into allies. This connection helps you see beyond your own world, opening doors to understanding.

Learn Empathy

So, how do you connect with empathy?

- Really listening: Put down your phone, look someone in the eye, and give them your full attention. It's about hearing not just the words but the emotions behind them.

- Think about people's points of view without judgment. It's like trying on a pair of glasses with a new prescription; you see things in a way you couldn't before.

- Ask open-ended questions that invite conversation rather than Yes/No questions. These questions show that you're not just waiting for your turn to talk but are really interested.

Imagine going to work at a place where team members understand each other's viewpoints. Trust grows, reducing misunderstandings and conflicts.

At home, these methods of conversing can turn a tense dinner table into a place of warmth and support. It strengthens bonds, creating a foundation of trust that encourages openness.

8.3 Empathy Gap: Learn to See Beyond Your Perspective

Imagine living in a city where the temperature varies widely throughout the year, ranging from bitterly cold winters to scorching hot summers. Now, picture two people: one has lived in this city their whole life, while the other has just moved from a tropical climate where the weather is consistently warm.

On a chilly winter day, the long-term resident might find the weather mildly uncomfortable but generally manageable because it fits their paradigm, and they're accustomed to it. However, the newcomer, unaccustomed to such cold, feels the chill deeply; it's painfully cold, almost unbearable.

The long-term resident might struggle to be empathetic, remarking, "It's not that cold; just put on another layer." They fail to recognize that what is a slight discomfort for them is a significant hardship for the newcomer.

This is **the empathy gap**: failing to understand how the same condition can be experienced so differently by someone else due to differing backgrounds, experiences, or personal thresholds. It's a chasm that forms when we fail to understand or connect with the emotions of those around us. It's like when an adult dismisses a teenager's painful breakup as only "puppy love".

This gap leads to miscommunication and disconnect, often leaving relationships stranded on rocky ground. When we fail to grasp people's emotional states or relate to their experiences, we miss out on the enjoyment of human connection. We become like ships passing in the night, each on our own course, missing the chance to share the journey.

The **root cause** of the empathy gap is that **assumptions take over** when you don't understand where someone is coming from. Have you ever had a heated debate because you made assumptions about what someone said?

Misunderstandings are common in the workplace, especially when cultural differences exist.

- Imagine a team meeting where someone from India asks about an American teammate's marital status, salary, age, or personal life. In many parts of India, these questions are seen as part of friendly, polite conversation, especially among new acquaintances. However, such questions might be perceived as invasive and inappropriate in the United States.

- For an American to express surprise at an Indian's fluent English can be offensive. English is one of the official languages of India, widely used in government, business, and media, and taught from a young age in many schools.

- Similarly, asking an Indian teammate to "say something in Indian" demonstrates a lack of awareness. India is a linguistically diverse country with numerous languages. It's more respectful to ask specifically about someone's native language.[17]

Consider a relationship where one partner's emotional needs go unnoticed because they're expressed differently. It's like speaking different languages without a translator; frustration occurs.

- Americans tend to express their needs and emotions explicitly, but French communication can be more nuanced and indirect. This difference can lead to an American partner missing subtle cues that a French partner believes are clear expressions of their needs or feelings.[18]

- Americans might approach conflict directly and expect a straightforward discussion to resolve issues. Germans might emphasize structure and formality in addressing disagreements, focusing more on thoroughness and correctness rather than a quick resolution. An American might interpret this as evasive or overly critical, whereas a German might view the American approach as rushing or lacking depth.[19]

SEE MORE CLEARLY

Overcoming the empathy gap isn't magic.

- Look for diverse viewpoints and experiences. Open yourself up to conversations and situations that challenge your usual mindset. It's like traveling to a new country and learning the customs; you gain a broader understanding of the world.

- Suspend judgment. Next time you're in a conversation, try muting your inner critic. It's easy to jump to conclusions, but instead, try to turn potential conflict into a learning opportunity. Listen to understand, not to respond.

- Participate in cultural competence workshops. These workshops offer insights into different cultural norms and practices, expanding your ability to understand.

- Reading literature from diverse authors is like opening a window into different worlds, allowing you to experience life through the eyes of characters from various backgrounds. These resources provide the perspective needed to bridge the empathy gap, making it easier to connect with people genuinely.

8.4 Emotional Labor: The Work of Supporting Other People's Feelings

Think about the last time you had to keep your composure while dealing with someone else's meltdown. That's **emotional labor** in action. It's the invisible work of managing your own emotions to keep everything around you running smoothly. It's like being the emotional janitor, constantly cleaning up after people's messes while trying to maintain harmony.

The term "emotional labor" is a buzzword for responsibilities that have always been a part of human interactions, like managing emotions or dealing with difficult people. You might view it as an overrated concept used to evade confrontation. Focusing on feelings that can hinder straightforward communication and decision-making may seem unnecessary.

For example, when it comes to changes in the workplace,

- You might think that efficiency and results should take precedence over emotions, and the traditional stiff-upper-lip approach to challenges is necessary for order and productivity.

- You might think that life requires a thick skin and an ability to proceed regardless of emotional undercurrents and that those unable to do so should toughen up rather than expect society to bend to their emotional needs.

However, emotional labor is not about *catering* to other people's feelings; it's about *supporting* teammates to work through those feelings. We learn in the practice of Change Management that this is a critical component of achieving peak productivity and efficiency in any professional setting.

> Change Management: The emotional labor of supporting teammates through change is critical in order to achieve the peak productivity desired from a workplace change.

Recognizing and effectively managing feelings can lead to a harmonious work environment, directly correlating with increased productivity and minimized conflict. It's about building a workplace where everyone can excel, unencumbered by avoidable emotional distress.[20]

Emotional labor encompasses skills required for **leadership**, such as empathy, emotional regulation, and the ability to inspire and motivate people. These skills are vital for team success, enhancing job satisfaction, and reducing employee turnover, all of which are key indicators of a thriving business environment.

On a personal level, the emotional labor of paying attention to feelings enhances your understanding of personal emotional triggers. It improves relationships by promoting better communication. This contributes to overall mental health and well-being.

8.5 Emotional Regulation Techniques

You're in a meeting, and things are heating up faster than a pressure cooker can pop its top. Voices rise, frustration mounts, and suddenly everyone's talking over each other. It's in moments like these that emotional regulation becomes crucial.

Emotional regulation is all about managing your emotions, especially when the pressure is on. It's like having a thermostat for your feelings, keeping them from boiling over inappropriately. This ability can make the difference between a constructive conversation and a full-blown argument in relationships. When you can regulate your emotions, you're less likely to escalate conflicts, creating a more stable environment for everyone around you.

Make It Better

So, how do you keep your cool when the world seems intent on provoking a toxic outburst?

- Step back and think about the situation. It's about being present and aware, not letting your emotions speak first. By taking the time to think, you can catch those emotional spikes before they erupt.

- Take a deep breath. It's a simple pause that I know really helps. When you feel your tension rising, take a moment to breathe deeply, with a slow inhale and exhale. It's like hitting the pause button on your emotional rollercoaster, allowing you to regroup before reacting.

Emotional regulation positively impacts relationships. You're less likely to lash out or retreat into silence when you manage your emotions effectively. It's about responding thoughtfully rather than reacting impulsively.

This kind of emotional resilience promotes positive interactions, reducing the likelihood of conflicts spiraling out of control.

- Suppose you're in a tense discussion with a colleague, and things escalate. Instead of matching their intensity, you pause and take a deep breath. This simple act can de-escalate the situation, allowing for a more reasoned discussion.

- Imagine a stressful day where everything seems to go wrong. Instead of succumbing to frustration, you focus on what you can control and find that cloud's silver lining.

These examples show how emotional regulation can pave the way for more constructive and harmonious relationships.

8.6 Recap and Check-in

As we wrap up our exploration of what popular psychology calls emotional intelligence (EI) and empathy, let's review what we've uncovered.

- We reviewed the four social skills that define EI: **self-awareness, self-regulation, social awareness, and relationship management**. EI is about knowing your own emotional landscape and navigating the emotions of other people with empathy and skill.

- We learned that connecting with empathy requires really listening, thinking about others' points of view without judgment, asking open-ended questions, and inviting conversation. These actions show that you're not just waiting for your turn to talk but are really interested.

- We defined the empathy gap with many examples, showing how limitations in your perspective can lead to assumptions that prevent you from even feeling empathy, much less showing it. We learned to find diverse viewpoints and experiences, suspend judgment, and try to turn potential conflict into a learning opportunity.

- We reviewed the benefits of emotional labor, managing our emotions and other's emotions for keeping harmony intact in our relationships. Making the effort can lead to a more productive workforce and a happier home life.

- We also tackled emotional regulation, emphasizing the need to manage our feelings, especially when the pressure mounts. Techniques like taking time to think and taking a deep breath help keep us calm when emotions threaten to boil over. By regulating our emotions, we avoid conflicts and pave the way for more meaningful connections.

Throughout this chapter, the focus has been on empathy: the ability to see the world through another's eyes. Regardless of its buzzword status, empathy is the glue that binds us, building understanding and trust.

A Pause for Thought

As someone who might not see themselves needing change, you may wonder if talking about feelings and empathy holds any value.

- Consider the impact of truly understanding the emotions of those around you.

- Imagine how relationships could shift if approached with a willingness to connect on a deeper level.

- Think about the workplace, where empathetic communication might turn colleagues into collaborators

- Think about home, where empathetic communication might turn family dinners into conversations filled with warmth and understanding.

- Ask yourself if recognizing and responding to the feelings of other people might improve your life. This might lead to better relationships than you thought possible.

In the next chapter, we'll explore how digital communication and artificial intelligence can impact our communication, sometimes provoking toxic responses.

See Appendix 1 if you'd like to work through some thought-provoking questions.

CHAPTER 9

DIGITAL COMMUNICATION AND AI IMPACT

Have you ever posted something online, and within seconds, a comment makes you think, "Wow, that escalated quickly?" This is the risk of digital communication, where anonymity and immediacy combine to create a breeding ground for toxic behavior.

9.1 THE ROLE OF DIGITAL COMMUNICATION IN MODERN TOXICITY

You're scrolling through social media, and out of nowhere, someone with a cartoon avatar starts finding fault with an innocent post that you "liked." It's all too common; troll culture and cyberbullying have found a home online, where people feel emboldened to say things they'd never dream of uttering face-to-face. In fact, a recent study found that 55% of teens have faced cyberbullying[21], illustrating just how pervasive this issue really is.

Why does this happen so easily online? The lack of non-verbal cues makes digital communication a minefield for misinterpretation. You send an email with the best intentions, and before you know it, you've accidentally offended someone because they read your "just the facts" message as abrasive. It's like trying to communicate with a robot that doesn't understand sarcasm. Without the nuances of tone, facial expressions, or body language, even the most innocent message can be misconstrued, leading to conflicts that never should have existed in the first place.

This digital world we navigate doesn't just affect our online interactions; it spills over into our personal and professional relationships. Email exchanges become battlegrounds where misunderstandings and conflicts thrive, often because we assume the worst about the sender's tone. It's like the old game of telephone, passing a message from person to person, where the message gets jumbled with each iteration.

Meanwhile, decreased face-to-face interaction weakens our bonds with people. When you can send a quick text instead of meeting up for coffee, those personal connections slowly wither away, leaving a void that no emojis can fill.

Digital platforms also amplify existing toxic behaviors. Think of them as a megaphone for misinformation and rumors, spreading them faster than you can say "fake news." In this echo chamber, where like-minded individuals reinforce each other's toxic statements, it becomes challenging to break free from negativity. As a result, toxic behaviors become entrenched, making online spaces feel more like hostile territories than places for open dialogue.

Make It Better

So, how do we combat this digital toxicity?

- Start by implementing clear communication guidelines for online platforms, whether it's at work or in group chats.

- Encourage respectful and constructive discourse, reminding people that behind every screen is a real person with feelings. It's not about censorship but building an environment where everyone feels safe to express themselves without fear of ridicule.

- Take that deep breath, then take the time to craft thoughtful responses rather than reacting impulsively. This pause can differentiate between escalating a situation and finding common ground.

A Pause for Thought

Take a moment to evaluate your digital habits.

- Are there platforms where you find yourself more prone to negativity?

- Do you often misinterpret messages due to lack of context?

- Consider scheduling regular breaks from screens or setting boundaries for online interactions.

- Think about how these changes can improve your relationships and mental health.

9.2 Navigate Online Interactions with Tact and Understanding

You're replying to an email or a social media comment, and your fingers are itching to fire back a quick response. But wait; this is where taking a breath and crafting a thoughtful reply can make a difference.

In the digital age, where speed gets you more attention, slowing down to consider the impact of your words can prevent regret. It's about thinking, "How would I feel if I received this message?" Thoughtful responses show you care and help avoid misunderstandings from hasty typing.

Emojis and tone indicators can be surprisingly effective, too. Who knew a tiny smiley face could soften the blow of a direct message? These small additions can convey warmth and intent, bridging the gap left by the absence of facial expressions and tone of voice.

Empathy is your secret angel in online interactions. It's not about gushing over every post with heart emojis but recognizing the human on the other side of the screen.

Every comment has a person behind it, someone with feelings and experiences. Maybe they're nice, or perhaps they like to argue. When you acknowledge and validate others' feelings in your comments and messages, you bring out their good side and create a space where real connection can happen.

This acknowledgment doesn't mean you agree with everything said, but it shows you're listening and respecting their perspective. It's like saying, "I see you, and I hear you," even in the vast digital realm. By recognizing their viewpoint, you can change potential conflicts into opportunities for understanding, making the online world a bit kinder and more connected.

Make It Better

Those inevitable online disagreements will happen; it's just the nature of the beast. But they don't have to spiral into toxic exchanges.

- One effective strategy is to take heated discussions to private messages. It's like moving a noisy bar conversation to a quiet corner, where you can hear each other better. This shift allows for more nuanced dialogue, reducing the chance of public escalation.

- Agreeing to disagree is another tool in your digital toolkit. Sometimes, despite your best efforts, you won't see eye to eye, and that's okay. Respectfully acknowledging this can diffuse tension and preserve relationships. It's about keeping things civil and focused on understanding rather than winning.

> Sometimes you won't see eye to eye. Agree to disagree.

Technology offers tools to enhance this online empathy, too.

Have you noticed an app suggesting adjustments to the tone of your message before it gets sent? I've seen that on the Nextdoor app. It's like having a digital editor who ensures your words come across as intended.

Browser extensions can also help, highlighting problematic language and offering alternatives.

- **Upful**: This browser extension is designed to detect biased language and suggest more inclusive alternatives in real time. It integrates with various web platforms commonly used in professional settings, helping to promote inclusivity and eliminate bias across communications. (Upful, 2023). https://www.upful.ai/product,

- **LanguageTool**: This writing assistant offers real-time grammar, style,

and tone checks in over 25 languages. It goes beyond basic spell-checking to detect complex language errors and suggest improvements. (LanguageTool, 2024).
https://chromewebstore.google.com/detail/ai-grammar-checker-paraph/oldceeleldhonbafppcapldpdifcinji

If you're looking to improve your digital communication skills further, online workshops or seminars can help. These resources provide structured guidance on navigating the complexities of online interactions, teaching you to communicate effectively and empathetically. They're like a crash course in digital diplomacy, equipping you with the skills for thoughtful engagement.

- **Coursera** offers a course titled "Improving Communication Skills," where you can learn how to communicate more effectively at work. This course is taught by an award-winning professor from the Wharton School, providing valuable insights and strategies. https://www.coursera.org/

- **Harvard University** provides multiple communication skills courses through its online platform. https://pll.harvard.edu/

- **Mind is the Master** offers various interactive online workshops to improve different elements of communication. https://www.mindisthemaster.com/

Incorporating these practices into your digital life might seem too complicated initially, but they can significantly improve your online interactions. By taking the time to craft considerate responses, recognize the human behind the screen, and manage disagreements constructively, you will avoid making posts you regret and contribute to a more positive digital environment.

9.3 AI for EI: Humanizing Technology

There was a time when the idea of robots helping us understand emotions seemed like something out of a sci-fi movie. But here we are, living in an age where **artificial intelligence (AI)** is stepping into the realm of **emotional intelligence**

(EI). It's like having a digital assistant who knows your schedule and senses when you're having a rough day.

AI-driven emotional analysis tools are changing the game. They can analyze text, tone, and even facial expressions to provide feedback on your emotional state. Imagine an AI tool that helps you realize that your seemingly neutral email might come across as cold. It's like having a friend gently nudge you to add a sprinkle of warmth to your message.

Virtual reality is another fascinating tool that can help you learn emotional intelligence. Imagine slipping into a VR headset and finding yourself in scenarios challenging your empathy.

- By walking in someone else's shoes to experience their world, these exercises can open our eyes to perspectives we might not have considered.

- They're like empathy workouts, stretching our understanding and compassion muscles in ways traditional methods can't.

- These experiences can be particularly powerful in educational settings, where they provide students with immersive lessons in empathy and cultural understanding.

With great power comes great responsibility. Integrating AI into emotional contexts brings up a host of challenges and ethical considerations.

- Privacy is a big concern. When AI tools collect emotional data, misuse or unauthorized access is risky. Imagine sharing your deepest feelings with an app, only to have that information fall into the wrong hands. It's a real concern requiring that developers code robust privacy protections.

- There's also the risk of becoming overly reliant on AI for emotional understanding. We might start leaning on AI interpretations instead of trusting our own instincts, losing touch with our human capacity for empathy and connection.

Despite these concerns, AI applications that can enhance interpersonal skills are undeniably promising.

- AI-powered chatbots, for instance, can offer real-time feedback on our communication style, pointing out areas where we might be coming off as too verbose or unprofessional. It's like having your own communication coach available 24/7.

- Emotion recognition software is another tool making waves, particularly in customer service. By analyzing facial expressions and vocal cues, these programs can guide representatives in responding more empathetically, improving customer interactions and satisfaction. It's as if AI provides a cheat sheet for reading the room, helping us navigate tricky conversations gracefully.

Complementing AI insights with **personal thought** is crucial to striking the right balance between technology and humanity. AI can offer valuable data, but we must interpret and apply it thoughtfully, considering the nuances that only human intuition can grasp.

Face-to-face interactions are still essential. While AI can enhance our emotional intelligence, nothing replaces the richness of in-person connections. It's like using a GPS to find your way but still stopping to ask a local person for insider tips.

By blending AI advancements with our innate human abilities, we can build a world where technology supports, rather than supplants, our emotional improvement.

9.4 Manage Digital Burnout: Set Boundaries in Your Connected World

Imagine waking up one morning, bleary-eyed, with the weight of a dozen notifications pressing down on you. Your phone is practically buzzing off the nightstand, demanding attention before you even have your morning coffee.

This is the modern-day reality of digital burnout. It's constant fatigue and exhaustion from endless screen time. It's when your eyes start to feel like they've been glued to a screen for hours (because they have), and your brain is running on empty. It's like trying to fill a cup that has a hole in the bottom; no matter how much you pour in, it never feels full.

SEE MORE CLEARLY

The effects of digital burnout go beyond physical fatigue. They also affect mental health and personal relationships.

- Imagine you've spent the entire day switching between video calls, emails, and social media, and by evening, you're so mentally drained that even the idea of a conversation feels overwhelming. You're present physically, but mentally you're somewhere else entirely.

- This lack of presence can strain personal relationships, creating a chasm between you and your loved ones.

- The constant barrage of digital engagement ramps up stress and anxiety levels, turning everyday life into a pressure cooker ready to explode.

- It's like being on a hamster wheel that never stops spinning, and you're left wondering how to jump off without landing flat on your face.

MAKE IT BETTER

Setting healthy digital boundaries is crucial in reclaiming your peace of mind.

- Start by scheduling regular digital detox periods, signaled with the phrases, "Screens Off" or "Devices Down". These are mini vacations from digital chaos, during which you unplug and recharge.

- Whether it's an hour a day or a full weekend, these breaks offer a much-needed respite, allowing your mind to rest and reset.

- Establishing no-screen zones or times at home can also make a difference. Imagine a dinner table free from the glow of screens, where conversations flow, and connections deepen.

- It's about creating spaces where you can be fully present without the incessant ping of notifications pulling you away.

Tools and techniques are at your disposal to help maintain a healthy digital balance.

- Apps that track and limit screen time usage can serve as digital guardians, nudging you to step away when you've hit your limit. They're like having a personal trainer but for your digital habits.

- Taking the time to relax and think can help. To counteract digital overload, incorporate moments of digital pause for restful thinking throughout your day.

- Simply walking outside can stabilize you in the present moment, providing a reality anchor in the digital storm.

While technology is a part of life, it doesn't have to consume it entirely. It's not about cutting ties with technology but learning to coexist with it in a way that enhances your quality of life. You can reclaim control over your life by recognizing the signs of digital burnout and addressing it.

> Technology is a part of life, but it doesn't have to consume it.

9.5 Recap and Check-in

As we wrap up this exploration of digital communication and its risks, you might be thinking about how these insights apply to your own screen-heavy life.

Digital platforms can both enrich and complicate our lives. They offer a stage for creativity and connection but invite misunderstandings and miscommunications that can lead to unnecessary conflict. It's the double-edged sword of the digital age. While the immediacy of online interactions brings us closer, it can also pull us apart when used carelessly.

AI and digital tools can help you understand and improve your interactions with people, but they should never replace the human touch. It's crucial to balance technological insights with personal thought, ensuring that our gadgets enhance rather than replace our innate ability to connect on a human level. The heart of empathy lies in genuine human interaction.

Digital burnout can creep up on us like the tide rising on your beach blanket. Those endless hours in front of screens can leave us drained and disconnected, impacting our well-being and relationships.

Setting healthy boundaries is key to maintaining a balanced digital life. Small changes like digital detoxes or "screens off" zones in your home can improve how you relate to the world around you, providing space for real connections to flourish. The goal isn't to shun technology but to use it wisely. By understanding its purpose and taking steps to manage its influence, you can create a more harmonious digital environment for yourself and those around you.

A Pause for Thought

Think about how technology supports or hinders your ability to communicate with people.

- Have you ever sent a quick message, only to realize later it was taken the wrong way?

- Have you mindlessly scrolled through social media instead of engaging in real conversations?

- Have you started to consider how you can reduce toxicity in your digital communications?

- Think about when, where, and how you can set boundaries for using digital technology.

In the grand scheme of things, technology is just a tool. How we wield it determines whether it builds bridges or barriers in our relationships.

See Appendix 1 if you'd like to work through some thought-provoking questions.

Chapter 10

Persevere to Thrive

E veryone has had experiences of learning and improving, whether it's mastering a new skill, improving at a sport, or getting better at a hobby. An ability to thrive through perseverance (also called a "growth mindset", a trendy buzzword) is simply the belief that such improvement is possible in many areas of our lives, not just those we are naturally good at.

> Improvement is possible in more areas than just those we are naturally good at.

This concept has scientific backing. Studies show that people who believe their abilities can be developed often achieve more than those who believe their abilities are fixed, because they invest more effort into learning and persist in facing challenges.[22].

It's about viewing effort as a path to mastery, not a sign of weakness. So, when faced with a challenge, you seize it as an opportunity to learn and improve instead of throwing in the towel.

10.1 Take on Challenges with Perseverance

Adopting an attitude of taking on challenges can lead to increased motivation, higher achievement, and better resilience. It's not just about feeling good; it's about finding ways to overcome obstacles and achieve goals.

While self-help concepts seem overly optimistic or vague, thriving through perseverance is about adopting a practical approach to learning and improvement grounded in personal effort and real outcomes.

Let's look at some real-life heroes who have embraced challenges and succeeded.

- **Thomas Edison:** His approach to inventing is often cited as a prime example of thriving through perseverance. Edison famously said, "I have not failed. I've just found 10,000 ways that won't work." His persistence in experimenting and learning from failures underscores a core principle of his persistence in learning.[23]

- **J.K. Rowling:** Before becoming one of the world's most famous authors, Rowling faced numerous rejections from publishers. Her success with the "Harry Potter" series came from her belief in her potential and refusal to give up despite early setbacks.[24]

- **Michael Jordan:** Often celebrated as one of the greatest basketball players ever, Jordan was cut from his high school basketball team. He credits his success to his willingness to fail and learn from mistakes, famously stating, "I've failed over and over and over again in my life. And that is why I succeed."[25]

- **Oprah Winfrey:** Her path to becoming a media mogul was fraught with personal and professional challenges. Oprah's perseverance is evident in her ability to change failures and setbacks into opportunities for learning, reshaping her career and impact on global media.[26]

- **Albert Einstein:** His curiosity and commitment to questioning established scientific beliefs led to groundbreaking discoveries in physics. Einstein's career is a testament to the idea that intelligence and ability are not fixed traits and that questioning and learning drive progress.[27]

These famous individuals show perseverance isn't just about working in an area you're naturally good at but pushing its boundaries and persisting despite the odds. They exemplify how believing in the possibility of effort and learning can lead to extraordinary achievements beyond just their talents.

Here are some scenarios of ordinary people who improved by embracing challenges.

- Let's start with a student struggling with math at the beginning of the school year. Instead of giving up, they welcomed the challenge, dedicating extra time to homework and getting help. By the end of the semester, their grades have improved, and they've discovered a newfound love for the logic of numbers.

- Next, consider an employee who's thrust into a new role requiring skills they've never used before. Instead of panicking, they view this as a chance to grow. They take courses, ask questions, and, over time, master the new skills.

These stories aren't fairy tales; they represent objective evidence that persevering through challenges can lead to amazing improvements.

Make It Better

So, how do you cultivate this amazing attitude?

- Start by reinterpreting challenges. Instead of thinking, "I can't do this," ask yourself, "Can I learn this? How can I push through it?" It's about switching from a defeatist attitude to one of curiosity and learning.

- Be patient during setbacks. Remember, nobody becomes an expert overnight. Stumbling and falling is okay; what matters is getting back up and trying again.

- Be kind to yourself, like you would treat a friend, and allow yourself to keep trying.

A Pause for Thought

- Think about a recent challenge you had and how you initially viewed it.

- Think about how persevering through the challenge could make a difference.

- Think about an older challenge you had, one where you developed new skills through effort and learning. Think about how progress often follows setbacks.

10.2 Overcome Resistance to Change

Change can be tricky. It's what we all claim to want, yet when it comes knocking, we often find ourselves clinging to what's familiar like a cat refusing to leave the sofa.

At the heart of this reluctance is fear of failure and the unknown. It's like standing at the edge of a cliff, knowing you're wearing a parachute but unsure if it will open.

Then there's the comfort of routine, the cozy blanket we wrap ourselves in to ward off the chill of uncertainty. Our habits are familiar and predictable and don't demand much from us. They whisper a reassurance of safety and security.

But here's the catch: our habits hold us back. When you lack confidence in your ability to change, it's easy to settle into these routines, convincing yourself that sticking with the status quo is somehow the better choice. This resistance to change acts like a concrete wall blocking your way. It stifles your potential, leaving you stuck in stagnation.

When we refuse to change, our personal and professional lives suffer. Opportunities for learning and improvement pass by like trains we never bother to catch.

- Imagine missing out on a career advancement because you were too afraid to learn a new skill. (Unfortunately, I did this.)

- Imagine letting a personal relationship plateau without commitment because you didn't want to have a difficult conversation.

- This kind of resistance limits your world, keeping you from the fulfillment that lies on the other side of change.

Make It Better

Overcoming resistance is entirely possible with a few steps.

- Set incremental goals. Think of it as dipping your toes in the water before taking the plunge. Breaking change into smaller, manageable steps makes the transition less scary.

- Give yourself a pat on the back for each small victory as you inch closer to your goal.

- Get support from peers or mentors. You want to have a morale booster by your side, reminding you that you can do this.

- Lean on those who have walked the path before you, drawing strength and wisdom from their experiences.

Embracing change, despite its challenges, can lead to significant personal and professional improvement. When you open yourself to change, you often find increased confidence in your ability to achieve your goals.

This newfound confidence encourages you to tackle even more significant challenges. You may stumble upon new skills and passions, reigniting a sense of purpose and optimism. Welcoming change is not just about surviving it; it's about thriving because of it.

10.3 The Role of Feedback Loops in Personal Development

Let's talk about feedback loops for personal development. Imagine you're driving to work on your usual route when the traffic gets thick and slows down. Your GPS tells you that you can save time by taking an alternate route. Regardless of whether you know the reason for the slowdown, you accept that recommendation and change your route. That's a feedback loop in action. It's the process of using feedback, good or bad, to inform and guide your future actions.

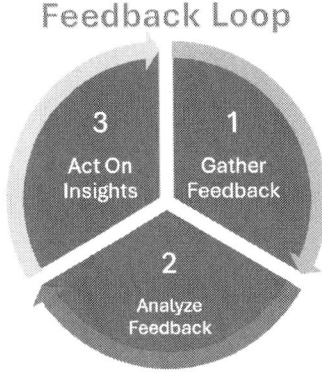

Feedback loops are like a personal GPS, recalculating your route to smoother roads. Instead of following the same old route, you've got a guide helping you navigate through the twists and turns of improvement.

Feedback loops strengthen your decision-making skills, turning guesswork into informed choices. Armed with feedback, you gain a clearer picture of your strengths and areas needing improvement. It's like having a mirror that shows not just your reflection but also the potential you hold. This awareness allows you to make better decisions and achieve your goals more efficiently.

Consider how feedback loops play out in real-world scenarios.

- Regular performance reviews at work offer insights that can lead to career advancement. They help you understand where you excel and where you need to improve.

- Consider an artist refining their work based on critiques, leading to a masterpiece.

- Similarly, iterative (agile) project methodologies rely on client feedback. You make ongoing improvements until the final piece matches what the client needs.

- In projects with defined work segments, feedback loops called "Lessons Learned" are used at the end of each work segment. These loops ensure that the team works well together and that the final product is not just satisfactory; it's a success.

Make It Better

So, how do you create effective feedback loops in your own life?

- Start by setting clear objectives and criteria for feedback. Whether it's a personal goal or a work project, knowing what you're aiming for helps you measure progress accurately.

- Encourage open and honest communication within your team or personal circles. Feedback should be a two-way street where everyone feels comfortable sharing and receiving insights. It's like having a conversation with a friend, where honesty and support go hand in hand.

- Remember, feedback isn't just about pointing out flaws; it's also about recognizing strengths and building upon them.

Incorporating feedback loops into your routine might seem awkward initially, but they can quickly become second nature. They offer a structured approach to improvement, ensuring you're always moving toward your goals.

As you welcome feedback, you'll find it becomes less about criticism and more about tactical ways to grow. It guides you not to become someone you're uncomfortable with but to become the best version of yourself.

10.4 Leverage Mistakes as Learning Opportunities

Mistakes. We've all made them, including the kind that keep you awake at night. Have you considered how those blunders could be steppingstones to something better? Mistakes are like those quirky teachers you had in school who seem harsh at first but teach life lessons that stick with you.

When you slip up, it's not just about what went wrong; it's about identifying areas where you can refine your skills. Mistakes made in a forgiving environment will encourage you to experiment and innovate, pushing boundaries to discover what works and doesn't. As we saw with the well-known people listed at the start of this chapter, mistakes are the trial runs that pave the way for success.

- Take the example of a tech company that launched a product only to find it wasn't hitting the mark. Instead of throwing in the towel, they listened to user feedback, tweaked the design, and released an improved version. Their willingness to learn from their mistakes led to a product that met and exceeded customer expectations.

- Consider a student who bombed an exam. Instead of sulking, they analyzed their errors, identified weak spots, and adjusted their study habits. Their next exam showed a marked improvement.

These examples highlight the power of learning from mistakes, turning setbacks into setups for future success.

Make It Better

Change how you look at mistakes so you can see learning opportunities.

- Start by analyzing what went wrong. Was it a lack of preparation? Overconfidence? (These both applied to a big mistake I made when I thought I knew the whole situation and didn't verify it.) Understanding the root cause can prevent you from making the same mistake twice.

- Own up to the mistake; don't make it worse by trying to hide or minimize it. (I quickly shared my mistake. Management forgave me and allocated time for the team to fix it.)

- Finally, try to appreciate the lesson you learned. Instead of dwelling on failure, focus on the knowledge gained. It's like finding a cloud's silver lining after a storm.

Resilience is the backbone of learning from mistakes. It's about developing a mindset of perseverance and determination. Think of it as mental toughness training, where each mistake strengthens your resolve.

> Resilience is mental toughness training;
> each mistake strengthens your resolve.

Having a supportive environment is helpful. You want to surround yourself with people who encourage you when the going gets tough. This will turn what could be a lonely road into a path filled with camaraderie and motivation. With resilience, mistakes become mere detours on the road to success, each teaching you how to navigate better.

A Pause for Thought

How do you react when you make mistakes?

- Do you hide it or act like it never happened?
- Do you persecute yourself?
- Do you feel remorse?

How do you react when other people make mistakes, such as your partner, child, or team member?

- Do you respond with toxic criticism? The silent treatment?
- Do you respond as though this mistake outweighs everything good about that person?
- Do you forgive and encourage them?

Think about how you responded to past mistakes, both your own and others' mistakes, and consider whether each response promoted learning and improvement.

10.5 The Long-term Benefits of Continually Improving

Picture life as a never-ending videogame of upgrades, where each level you conquer opens to new possibilities and rewards. That's the essence of continuous improvement, a commitment to continually enhance skills, refine processes, and achieve better outcomes. It's like subscribing to a lifelong learning channel, where the content keeps you engaged and evolving.

This approach isn't about drastic makeovers but minor, consistent tweaks that lead to big changes over time. By adopting a desire to continually improve, you ensure that each day is a little better than the day before.

This mindset of continually improving doesn't just apply to *people* learning; it also extends to *companies* where processes are fine-tuned, and outcomes are continually optimized. (I remember many years ago when Lowe's, the home improvement retailer, adopted an advertising slogan of "Never Stop Improving". The double negatives of "Never" and "Stop" seemed less than motivating to me. "Keep On Improving" seems more logical, but I don't know the rules of slogans and advertising.)

The advantage of continually improving is its long-term benefits. Adopting this mindset is like having a secret weapon that makes you adaptable to any situation life throws your way. Being flexible is like having a superpower in a world where change is the only constant.

> **Being adaptable is like having a superpower in a world where change is the only constant.**

Continuing to improve ensures you're not just keeping up but staying ahead of the curve, ready to tackle whatever comes next. There's an immense joy in knowing that you're growing and evolving, not because you have to, but because you want to.

Let's consider some real-world scenarios.

- Think about a professional who climbs the career ladder through ongoing education and skill enhancement. They don't wait for opportunities to knock; they create them by staying informed and updated. They ensure their skills are always sharp by attending workshops, earning certifications, or even reading industry-related articles.

- Or take an organization that achieves operational excellence through regular process reviews. They don't settle for good enough; they strive for greatness by continually evaluating and refining their operations.

This commitment to improvement doesn't just boost efficiency; it promotes innovation and sets a standard of excellence.

Make It Better

So, how do you build this culture of continually improving?

- Start by setting regular goals with interim milestones. These act like signposts on your journey, guiding you toward learning and development. Whether learning a new language or mastering a skill, having clear goals keeps you focused and motivated.

- Find new challenges and learning opportunities. Welcome uncertainty and step out of your comfort zone. It's in these spaces of uncertainty that true learning happens.

- Remember, continually improving isn't a destination; it's a way of living. It's about waking up each day with a curious mind, ready to learn and grow in ways you never imagined.

10.6 Recap and Check-in

This chapter has been a journey through the powerful concepts of embracing change, learning from mistakes, and continually improving. These elements contribute to a mindset that refuses to be stagnant, constantly pushing boundaries to pursue personal and professional learning. It's about seeing setbacks not as failures but as opportunities to stretch.

Think back to feedback loops and how they serve as your personal GPS, guiding you toward your goals with precision. The advantage of these loops lies in their simplicity: assess, analyze, and adjust. They allow you to steer your own ship rather than being tossed around by the waves of uncertainty.

Likewise, learning from mistakes can be life changing. Instead of fearing failure, you learn to welcome it as an integral part of the improvement process. It's about finding success through a myriad of lessons learned along the way.

Continuous improvement becomes the thread that ties all these concepts together. By committing to lifelong learning, you enrich your own life plus the lives of those around you. You set goals, welcome challenges, and never settle for the status quo. This pursuit of learning becomes a habit, a part of who you are. It's less about the destination and more about the evolving journey, leading to greater satisfaction.

A Pause for Thought

Consider the application of these concepts to your own behaviors and interactions.

- Have you been nodding along, recognizing areas of your life where becoming receptive to change could improve things?

- Are there parts of your work or personal life that could benefit from a shift in perspective, a tweak here, or a nudge there?

- This chapter was about challenging the inertia and skepticism that may have held you back and daring to explore the possibilities beyond your comfort zone.

- Could deciding to thrive through perseverance help prevent some of the toxicity you've encountered or contributed to?

> Challenge the skepticism that has held you back.
> Dare to explore the possibilities beyond your comfort zone.

See Appendix 1 if you'd like to work through some thought-provoking questions.

Conclusion

I'm impressed that you stuck with me to the end! Let's look back at the journey we've taken together.

- We've explored the world of toxic behaviors, peeled back their layers, and explored their impact at work and home.

- We've identified those sneaky traits, like a relative's passive-aggressive comments or that colleague who turns every meeting into a gripe session.

- We've tackled microaggressions, gaslighting, and even the exhausting realm of toxic positivity.

- We've navigated the complexities of digital communication and the influence of AI, arming you with strategies for building healthier interactions.

- You've learned how to recognize and address these behaviors in other people and within yourself.

- We've journeyed through the root causes of toxicity, like learned behaviors and elevated self-perception.

- Together, we've unpacked tools for thinking about yourself, reviewed the importance of perseverance in learning, and explored how empathy can improve relationships digitally and in the real world.

Here's the exciting part: You've moved past your skepticism and come up with some ideas on how to try out the techniques you've learned. If you don't remember what you read, then take a look at Appendix 1 for thought-provoking questions and Appendix 2 for lists, followed by a request for a review.

Remember, it's not about perfection; it's about progress. By recognizing toxic behaviors and stepping away from them, you're opening the door to a healthier, more fulfilling life. You're not just improving your own experience but also enriching the lives of those around you.

Writing this book has been a labor of love, bringing my journey away from toxicity full circle. Your willingness to explore these themes and challenge yourself shows your openness to a healthier way of interacting, and that's worth celebrating.

Keep your momentum going through learning, demonstrating empathy, or just paying attention in your interactions. You're not alone in this. There's a whole world out there of people who are on similar journeys, and together, we can create a more understanding and less toxic world.

Thank you for your time, your openness, and your courage. I'm cheering you on every step of the way.

Delia Sikes

Appendix 1: Follow-Up Exercises

APPENDIX 1: FOLLOW-UP EXERCISES

Use these exercises to follow up on what you learned in this book.

CHAPTER 1: RECOGNIZE TOXIC BEHAVIOR

1. Use the 3 questions to assess whether a specific behavior is toxic. (Section 1.1, Appendix 2)

2. Evaluate your workplace for the presence of specific types of toxic behavior. (Sections 1.2 – 1.6 and 2.2 – 2.4, or Appendix 2)

3. Are you experiencing or causing gaslighting? Do something about it. (Section 1.5)

4. Are your actions helpful or harmful? Be more aware. (Section 1.7)

CHAPTER 2: THE IMPACT OF TOXIC BEHAVIOR AT HOME AND WORK

1. Evaluate your relationships that have been damaged by your toxicity. (Section 2.1)

2. Assess your parenting styles and evaluate whether your children have been impacted by your toxicity. (Section 2.2)

3. Assess your workplace and implement the ideas you've learned. (Section 2.3)

4. Implement the emotional connection techniques. (Section 2.4)

CHAPTER 3: DIGGING DEEPER INTO ROOT CAUSES

1. Write down interactions that don't go well, and think about what ingrained pattern might have triggered your toxic reaction. (Section 3.1)

2. Observe your current reactions and evaluate them for behaviors learned in childhood. (Section 3.1)

3. Assess whether you have insecurities that might be driving your behavior. (Section 3.2)

4. Evaluate yourself for whether you have an elevated self-perception. (Section 3.3)

5. Work on your insensitivity by noticing non-verbal cues and asking whether everything is OK. (Section 3.4)

6. Assess whether you're suffering stress and burnout. Implement time management, prioritization and relaxation. (Section 3.5)

CHAPTER 4: OVERCOMING SKEPTICISM TO WELCOME PERSONAL CHANGE

1. Consider a change you want to make, and assess where you are in the stages of change. Evaluate how you will get to the next stage. (Section 4.2)

2. What are your motivating reasons to change your behavior? (Section 4.3)

3. Do you have a fear of change? Try the tools learned: Focus, Baby Steps, a Positive Perspective, Flexibility, and Recognize Progress. (Section 4.4)

CHAPTER 5: LOOKING INWARD FOR SKEPTICS

1. Assess your past decisions and your paradigms for blind spots. (Section 5.1)

2. Do you struggle to get promoted? Do you have a frustrated partner? Get feedback on your attitude. (Section 5.1)

3. Create a personal SWOT analysis to assess your Strengths, Weaknesses, Opportunities and Threats. Make a plan to act on that information. (Section 5.2)

4. Have you scheduled an recurring meeting with yourself to relax and think about things? Make it a habit. (Section 5.3)

5. Identify your triggers – those things that cause a knee-jerk toxic reaction. (Section 5.5)

6. Think about what your personal values are and whether your actions align with those values. Consider whether the values need to change or your actions do. (Section 5.6)

7. Have you posted a review for this book? Please do. (See "Help Us Promote Understanding," between chapters 5 and 6.)

Chapter 6: Improve Communication Skills

1. Try using the techniques for really listening actively. (Section 6.1)

2. Do you know the secret to being Assertive instead of Aggressive? Use "I" statements. Try this out. (Section 6.2)

3. If you struggle with receiving feedback, select a technique to try. (Section 6.3)

4. Analyze body language for non-verbal communication – yours and others. Are the words and body language aligned with each other? (Section 6.4)

Chapter 7: Manage Conflict Constructively

1. What 2 techniques can you use to diffuse an escalating argument? Pause, and really listen actively. (Section 7.1)

2. Dig into your recurring surface-level conflicts to find their root causes. (Section 7.2)

3. Negotiation: Do you try to win at all costs? To compromise with give-and-take? To collaborate for a win/win solution? Try to compromise or collaborate on your next dispute. (Sections 7.3 – 7.4)

4. Would establishing boundaries head off some of your toxic triggers? Make a plan to implement a boundary and explain why. (Section 7.5)

5. What lessons can you learn from your conflicts? (Section 7.6)

CHAPTER 8: EI AND EMPATHY: REALITY BEHIND THE BUZZWORDS

1. Evaluate which EI skills you're good at and which could use some improvement. (Section 8.1)

   - Self-Awareness: Understanding yourself

   - Self-Regulation: Managing your emotions

   - Social Awareness: tuning into the emotional currents of those around you

   - Relationship Management: using that awareness to promote positive interactions

2. Assess yourself for emotional biases: Have you made any decisions that defied logic? (Section 8.1)

3. Think about how really listening and empathy can improve your relationships. (Section 8.2)

4. Think about a time when your lack of awareness led to assumptions that created an awkward empathy gap. How could you have avoided making assumptions? (Section 8.3)

5. Does your workplace use Change Management processes to help employees deal with change? If not, seek education and advocate for it. (Section 8.4)

6. Have you had to maintain your composure during someone else's meltdown? Are you capable of doing that? (Sections 8.4 – 8.5)

CHAPTER 9: DIGITAL COMMUNICATION AND AI IMPACT

1. Have you responded toxically on social media? Do you know how to ward off that behavior? Pause and question yourself before responding, and imagine saying those words to a real person face-to-face. (Sections 9.1 – 9.2)

2. When and where do you intentionally turn off your electronic devices? Consider establishing times and zones for doing that. Engage in more face-to-face conversations or spend the time thinking. (Section 9.4)

Chapter 10: Persevere to Thrive

1. Think about your past challenges. Did you persevere or give up? What could have made a difference? (Section 10.1)

2. Are you resistant to change? Evaluate how you can overcome that resistance. (Section 10.2)

3. Does your workplace use feedback loops, like Lessons Learned? How can you adopt that process at both work and home? (Section 10.3)

4. How do you react when you make mistakes? How do you react when other people make mistakes? Do you need to be more forgiving and promote learning from mistakes? (Section 10.4)

5. Are you actively improving yourself through learning? What will you focus on learning? (Section 10.5)

6. Have you posted a review for this book? Please do. (See "Help Us End Toxic Behavior," after Appendix 2)

Appendix 2: Lists

APPENDIX 2: LISTS

The numbers shown in parentheses reference the section where the topic is discussed.

Types of Toxicity

1. Persistent negativity (1.1)

2. Manipulative communication tactics (1.1)

3. Failure to respect boundaries (1.1)

Red Flags

These are categories of toxic behaviors that fall under the 3 types listed above.

1. Passive-aggressiveness (1.2, 2.1)

2. Sarcasm wrapped in a thin layer of humor (1.2)

3. Deliberate procrastination (1.2)

4. Veiled criticism masked as a joke (1.2)

5. Office bully (1.2)

6. Chronic complainers (1.2)

7. Constant need for validation (1.2)

8. Defensiveness (1.2, 1.3)

9. Manipulation: Withholding information (1.2), exclusion from meetings (2.3), by parents (2.2)

10. Road Rage (1.2)

11. Guilt tripping (1.3)

12. The silent treatment (1.3)

13. Gaslighting (1.3, 1.5)

14. Blame shifting / deflection (1.3)

15. Minimizing personal faults while exaggerating other's (1.3)

16. Overbearing / insisting on your own way (1.3)

17. Bias (stereotyping) microaggression (1.4)

18. Toxic positivity (1.6)

19. Lack of Emotional Support by parents (2.2)

20. Inappropriate Boundaries by parents (2.2)

21. Abuse: physical, emotional or psychological (2.2)

22. High Conflict and Instability (2.2)

23. Constant criticism (2.2)

24. Neglect by parents (2.2)

25. Conditional Love by parents (2.2)

26. Ruling with fear and intimidation (2.3)

27. Micromanagement (2.3)

28. Making arbitrary demands (2.3)

29. Lack of concern for people's feelings (2.4)

Tests for Toxic Behavior

Ask these questions to determine if a particular behavior is toxic. (1.1)

1. Does it repeatedly harm others?

2. Is it intended to control or manipulate?

3. Does it consistently breach mutual respect?

EFFECTS AT WORK AND HOME

1. Emotional disconnection (2.4)

2. Numbness / unwilling to engage / a wall of defense (2.4)

3. Damage to a child's emotional, cognitive and physical development (2.2)

4. Loss of productivity and team creativity (2.3)

5. Resentment (2.3)

6. Ending the relationship: Turnover or Separation (2.4)

ROOT CAUSES

1. Learned behaviors (3.1)

2. Insecurity (3.2)

3. Elevated Self-Perception (3.3)

4. Insensitivity and Apathy (3.4)

5. Stress and Burnout (3.5)

POP PSYCHOLOGY BUZZWORDS & THEIR ALTERNATE WORDS USED IN THIS BOOK FOR SELF-HELP SKEPTICS

- Active Listening: Really listening, being engaged
- Celebrate: Appreciate
- Continuous Improvement: continually improving
- Deep Breathing: Taking a deep breath

- Echo Chamber effect: Being surrounded by "Yes" men, rubber stampers
- Embrace: Welcome
- Empathy: You can see things from another person's perspective, Understanding
- Foster: Build, promote, leads to
- Grounding: Stabilizing
- Growth Mindset: Thriving through perseverance
- Growth: Improvement, Learning
- Journaling: Write it down
- Meditation: Think only about one thing or nothing at all
- Mindfulness: Pay attention and think only about the present moment
- Mindset: Perspective
- Opportunities for Growth: Opportunities to learn
- Personal Transformation: Personal change
- Reflect on: Think about
- Reflection: Thought
- Reflects: Represents
- Reframing: Changing how you look at it, Reinterpreting
- Resilience: Ability to bounce back from adversity
- Self-awareness: Understanding yourself
- Self-Compassion: Be kind to yourself

- Self-Help: Personal development, self-improvement, self-care, self-guidance, self-enhancement

- Self-Reflection: Thinking about yourself, Looking inward

- Self-regulation: Managing your emotions

- Subconscious: Intuition, Gut feeling

- Therapist: Coach

- Transform: Change

- Transformation: Improvement

Help Us End Toxic Behavior

"Everything that irritates us about others can lead us to an understanding of ourselves." Carl Jung

Have you learned ways to stop toxic behavior? Before you close this book, imagine helping someone just like you, someone who is skeptical of typical self-help advice but is open to genuine, evidence-based insights into changing behaviors.

We aim to challenge misconceptions and promote a more thoughtful approach to stop toxic behavior. We want to reach as many minds as possible and need your candid feedback.

Your voice is powerful. Many people decide which books to read based on recommendations like yours. Since you've reached the end of this book, I'm asking you to leave a review for ***I'm Not Toxic, You're Overreacting***.

Leaving a review is a straightforward act that takes just a moment but can have a significant impact. Your insights can:

- Help one more person recognize and modify unhelpful behaviors.
- Help one more professional enhance their workplace interactions.
- Help one more individual improve their personal relationships.
- Help one more family member understand and address toxic dynamics.
- Help one more story of change begin.

Are you ready to encourage more conversation about toxic behavior? It's simple! Go to this book in your media purchases, and leave your review with a rating, a video or photo, and your honest thoughts. Links and instructions vary based on which media type you're reading, so details are provided below.

With sincere thanks,

Delia Sikes

To review **the eBook** of ***I'm Not Toxic, You're Overreacting***, **please click the appropriate link for your country**. If your country isn't listed, please find the order in your Amazon media purchases.

US: https://www.amazon.com/review/review-your-purchases/?asin=B0F6KTQLDL

Canada: https://www.amazon.ca/review/review-your-purchases/?asin=B0F6KTQLDL

UK: https://www.amazon.co.uk/review/review-your-purchases/?asin=B0F6KTQLDL

Australia: https://www.amazon.com.au/review/review-your-purchases/?asin=B0F6KTQLDL

To review **the paperback book** of *I'm Not Toxic, You're Overreacting*, **please scan the appropriate QR code for your country.** If your country isn't listed, please find the order in your Amazon media purchases.

To review **the hardcover book** of *I'm Not Toxic, You're Overreacting*, **please scan the appropriate QR code for your country.** If your country isn't listed, please find the order in your Amazon media purchases.

HELP US END TOXIC BEHAVIOR

Review Hardcover in US

Review Hardcover in Canada

Review Hardcover in UK

Review Hardcover in Australia

In the Audible app,) click the 3 dots by the book in your library listing and select Rate and Review.

Remember that sharing knowledge is one of the best ways to build relationships. If this book has helped you, consider passing it on to someone who might benefit.

To purchase **the paperback book** of ***I'm Not Toxic, You're Overreacting*** *for someone you know who has toxic tendencies,* **please click the appropriate link or scan the QR code for your country.** If your country isn't listed, please search for the title.

US: https://www.amazon.com/dp/1967134065

Canada: https://www.amazon.ca/dp/1967134065

UK: https://www.amazon.co.uk/dp/1967134065

Australia: https://www.amazon.com.au/dp/1967134065

Endnotes

1. *Toxic Workplace Checklist: 14 Signs to Look Out For* https://business.talkspace.com/articles/toxic-workplace-checklist

2. *Toxic Workplace Checklist: 14 Signs to Look Out For* https://business.talkspace.com/articles/toxic-workplace-checklist

3. Parentification is a process where a child assumes roles and responsibilities that are typically fulfilled by a parent. This often involves taking care of siblings or managing household duties beyond what is appropriate for their age. The child may also provide emotional support to the parent(s), which can reverse the typical caregiving dynamic. Parentification can lead to a range of emotional and psychological effects, both positive and negative, depending on the context and extent of the responsibilities assumed by the child.

4. Kerr, M. E., & Bowen, M. (1988). *Family evaluation: An approach based on Bowen theory*. New York, NY: W. W. Norton & Company.

5. Evans, G. W., Li, D., & Whipple, S. S. (2013). Cumulative risk and child development. *Psychological Bulletin, 139*(6), 1342-1396.

6. Cognitive-behavioral techniques are therapeutic strategies that focus on identifying and modifying dysfunctional patterns in thought and behavior. These techniques are grounded in the principle that psychological problems are partly based on faulty or unhelpful ways of thinking and learned patterns of unhelpful behavior. Individuals can improve their mental health and overall functioning by changing these negative thought patterns and behaviors. Therapists using these techniques help individuals challenge their negative thoughts, assess their validity, and replace them with more accurate and beneficial ones. These interventions aim to alleviate symptoms of mental disorders and increase a person's ability to function effectively by fostering greater resilience and more adaptive coping mechanisms.

7. Hofmann, S. G., Asnaani, A., Vonk, I. J. J., Sawyer, A. T., & Fang, A. (2012). The efficacy of cognitive behavioral therapy: A review of meta-analyses. *Cognitive Therapy and Research, 36*(5), 427-440. This study offers a comprehensive review of meta-analyses examining the efficacy of cognitive-behavioral therapy (CBT) for a variety of disorders, including anxiety and depression. The findings from these analyses consistently show that CBT is highly effective in reducing symptoms associated with these mental health challenges, thus substantiating the claim that cognitive-behavioral interventions can serve as critical support for individuals suffering from anxiety and depression.

8. Cognitive-behavioral therapy (CBT) has been extensively studied and shown to be effective in helping individuals overcome specific phobias, including fear of flying and public speaking. Heimberg, R. G., Becker, R. E., Goldfinger, K., & Vermilyea, J. A. (1987). Treatment of social phobia by exposure, cognitive restructuring, and homework assignments. *Journal of Nervous and Mental Disease, 175*(6), 355-364. This study addresses the effectiveness of CBT techniques, particularly exposure therapy and cognitive restructuring, in treating social phobia, which often includes public speaking anxiety. It demonstrates how CBT helps individuals manage and eventually overcome their fears by changing their thought patterns and behaviors through guided exposure and skill training. Tortella-Feliu, M., Bornas, X., Llabrés, J., & Noguera, M. (2001). Computer-assisted exposure versus live graded exposure for fear of flying. *American Journal of Psychotherapy, 55*(4), 462-477. This study explores the use of computer-assisted and live exposure therapy, both under the umbrella of cognitive-behavioral interventions, to treat fear of flying. The results show significant improvements in individuals' ability to manage and reduce their flying-related phobia. Both studies illustrate the broader efficacy of CBT in treating various specific phobias, supporting the claim made in the sentence.

9. Doidge, N. (2007). *The brain that changes itself: Stories of personal triumph from the frontiers of brain science*. New York, NY: Viking. In this book, Norman Doidge provides extensive insights into how neuroplasticity underpins the brain's remarkable ability to adapt and reorganize itself in response to different experiences, in turn supporting personal transformation. This work is well-cited in discussions about how understanding and leveraging neuroplasticity can significantly change behavior and cognitive function.

10. The Stages of Change model, also known as the Transtheoretical Model of Change, was developed by James Prochaska and Carlo DiClemente in the late 1970s. Prochaska, J. O., & DiClemente, C. C. (1983). Stages and processes of self-change of smoking: Toward an integrative model of change. *Journal of Consulting and Clinical Psychology, 51*(3), 390-395. This paper presents the foundational concept of the Stages of Change model, outlining the various phases through which an individual progresses when attempting to change a behavior, including pre-contemplation, contemplation, preparation, action, and maintenance. It's a seminal work that provides a comprehensive theoretical framework for understanding the complexities of personal change.

11. One of the foundational references for goal-setting theory, particularly emphasizing the importance of setting specific and challenging goals to enhance performance, is by Edwin A. Locke and Gary P. Latham. A key publication from these authors that you can cite is: Locke, E. A., & Latham, G. P. (1990). *A theory of goal setting & task performance*. Englewood Cliffs, NJ: Prentice Hall. This book provides an in-depth discussion of goal-setting theory, detailing how clear, challenging goals contribute to enhanced task performance by focusing attention, mobilizing effort, increasing persistence, and fostering the development of strategies and action plans. This work is seminal in the field of organizational psychology and is widely referenced in discussions about motivation and achieving personal effectiveness through specific and structured goal setting.

12. A cognitive bias is a systematic pattern of deviation from norm or rationality in judgment, whereby inferences about other people and situations may be illogical. Individuals create their own "subjective reality" from their perception of the input. An individual's construction of reality, not the objective input, may dictate their behavior in the world. Thus, cognitive biases may sometimes lead to perceptual distortion, inaccurate judgment, illogical interpretation, or what is broadly called irrationality. These biases result from our brain's attempt to simplify information processing. They are often a result of the brain's attempt to save effort or reach quick conclusions, but they can also be influenced by emotions and social interactions. Cognitive biases can impact our decisions and behaviors in many areas, including financial decisions, interpersonal relationships, and our beliefs about the world.

13. The "bias blind spot" is defined as the cognitive bias of recognizing the impact of biases on the judgment of others while failing to see the impact of biases on one's own judgment. Essentially, it refers to people's tendency to believe they are less biased than others. This concept highlights an individual's inability to detect biases in their own thinking, even while they can often easily identify them in others' decisions and reasoning processes.

14. Cognitive dissonance is a psychological concept referring to the mental discomfort experienced by a person who holds two or more contradictory beliefs, ideas, or values at the same time or is confronted by new information that conflicts with existing beliefs, ideas, or values. This discomfort leads individuals to seek consistency among their cognitions (i.e., beliefs and attitudes), which often results in changes to attitudes, beliefs, or behaviors to reduce the discomfort and achieve consonance. Leon Festinger, who developed the theory in 1957, suggested that people have an inner drive to hold all their attitudes and beliefs in harmony and avoid disharmony (or dissonance). This is evident when people change their beliefs or behaviors in the face of conflicting evidence or discomfort from a contradiction between beliefs and actions. Festinger, L. (1957). *A theory of cognitive dissonance*. Stanford, CA: Stanford University Press. This book is where Leon Festinger first introduced the theory of cognitive dissonance, providing foundational insights into how conflicts between cognitions can drive changes in attitudes, beliefs, or behaviors.

15. As described, the distinction between hearing and listening captures essential differences in how we process sounds and information. Hearing is the physiological ability to perceive sound; it occurs when sound waves are converted into electrical signals that can be interpreted by the brain. It is generally considered a passive activity because it happens automatically without conscious effort. On the other hand, listening is an active process that requires attention and cognitive engagement. It involves hearing the sound and focusing on it, interpreting it, and making sense of it. Effective listening requires effort to understand the meaning of the words and the intent behind them, which is crucial in effective communication. VeryWellMind, a trusted resource for mental health information, explains these concepts clearly. Cherry, K. (2021, April 20). What's the difference between hearing and listening? *VeryWellMind*. https://www.verywellmind.com/hearing-vs-listening-what-s-the-difference-5196734

16. Salovey, P., & Mayer, J. D. (1990). Emotional Intelligence. *Imagination, Cognition, and Personality*, 9(3), 185-211.

17. Morrison, T., & Conaway, W. A. (2006). *Kiss, Bow, or Shake Hands: How to Do Business in Sixty Countries*. Avon, MA: Adams Media. This book provides insights into the business and communication practices in India compared to the U.S., highlighting the high-context nature of Indian communication versus Americans' low-context, direct communication style.

18. Wurtz, E. (2005). A cross-cultural analysis of websites from high-context cultures and low-context cultures. *Journal of Computer-Mediated Communication, 11*(1), 13-38. This study provides an understanding of how high-context communication (common in French culture) differs fundamentally from low-context communication (typical in American culture), particularly in non-verbal cues and indirect expressions.

19. Hall, E. T., & Hall, M. R. (1990). *Understanding cultural differences: Germans, French, and Americans*. Yarmouth, ME: Intercultural Press. This book delves into the contrasting communication styles and values of Germans and Americans, highlighting differences in expressiveness, approach to conflict, and expectations in personal and professional interactions.

20. Ashkanasy, N. M., Zerbe, W. J., & Härtel, C. E. J. (Eds.). (2000). *Emotions in the workplace: Research, theory, and practice*. Westport, CT: Quorum Books. This collection explores the role of emotions and emotional labor in organizational settings, discussing how effectively managing emotions can enhance employee performance and productivity.

21. *2023 Cyberbullying Data* https://cyberbullying.org/2023-cyberbullying-data

22. *Carol Dweck: A Summary of Growth and Fixed Mindsets* https://fs.blog/carol-dweck-mindset/

23. Josephson, Matthew. *Edison: A Biography*. Wiley, 1992.

24. Rowling, J.K. "The Fringe Benefits of Failure, and the Importance of Imagination." Commencement Speech, Harvard University, 2008.

25. Lazenby, Roland. *Michael Jordan: The Life*. Little, Brown and Company, 2014.

26. Kelley, Kitty. *Oprah: A Biography*. Crown Archetype, 2010.

27. Isaacson, Walter. *Einstein: His Life and Universe*. Simon & Schuster, 2007.

REFERENCES

- *Microaggressions: The impact on physical and mental health*
  https://www.medicalnewstoday.com/articles/microaggressions-how-and-why-do-they-impact-health

- *5 Go-To Tactics of Gaslighters, and How to Resist Them*
  https://www.psychologytoday.com/us/blog/the-mindful-self-express/202106/5-go-tactics-gaslighters-and-how-resist-them

- *How to Distinguish Healthy Positivity From Toxic Positivity*
  https://www.schoolofcoachingmastery.com/coaching-blog/how-to-distinguish-healthy-positivity-from-toxic-positivity

- *Toxic Relationships: The Experiences and Effects ...*
  https://pmc.ncbi.nlm.nih.gov/articles/PMC9527357/

- *How Toxic Organizational Culture Can Cost Your Business -*
  https://ccy.com/how-toxic-organizational-culture-can-cost-your-business/

- *Signs of Emotional Disconnection in a Relationship*
  https://www.therapyroute.com/article/signs-of-emotional-disconnection-in-a-relationship

- *The Effects of Leadership Styles and Organizational ...*
  https://www.sciencedirect.com/science/article/pii/S1877042811015606

06

- *Effects of positive and negative childhood experiences on ...*
  https://bmcpublichealth.biomedcentral.com/articles/10.1186/s12889-021-10732-w

- *Narcissism in the Workplace: Strategies for Management ...*
  https://www.therapynowsf.com/blog/narcissism-in-the-workplace

- *Stress, burnout linked to toxic workplace behaviors | Business*
  https://times-journal.com/business/article_3846a622-9386-11ed-ae9c-cb48465a4883.html

- *How to be more empathetic: 8 exercises to develop empathy*
  https://www.calm.com/blog/how-to-be-more-empathetic

- *Bias Blind Spot | Definition, Causes & Examples - Lesson*
  https://study.com/academy/lesson/bias-blind-spot-definition-examples.html

- *Don't Underestimate the Power of Self-Reflection*
  https://hbr.org/2022/03/dont-underestimate-the-power-of-self-reflection

- *Build your emotional vocabulary*
  https://www.workplacestrategiesformentalhealth.com/resources/build-your-emotional-vocabulary

- *Wheel of Emotions, Idaho State University*
  https://www.isu.edu/media/libraries/counseling-and-testing/documents/Wheel-of-Emotions-Handout-(3).pdf

- *Cognitive Dissonance: Definition and Examples*
  https://www.verywellmind.com/what-is-cognitive-dissonance-2795012

- *Cherry, K. (2021, April 20). What's the difference between hearing and listening? VeryWellMind.*
  https://www.verywellmind.com/hearing-vs-listening-what-s-the-differenc

e-5196734

- *Assertive Communication: Definition, Examples, and Tips*
  https://www.coursera.org/articles/assertive-communication

- *The Importance Of The Employee Feedback Loop*
  https://www.forbes.com/sites/forbescommunicationscouncil/2018/08/01/the-importance-of-the-employee-feedback-loop/

- *Understanding nonverbal communication - MSU Extension*
  https://www.canr.msu.edu/news/understanding_nonverbal_communication

- *4 Triggers Cause the Majority of Team Conflicts*
  https://hbr.org/2022/05/conflict-is-not-always-bad-but-you-should-know-how-to-manage-it

- *De-escalation techniques and resources | TMLT Resource Hub*
  https://hub.tmlt.org/tmlt-blog/de-escalation-techniques-and-resources

- *Effective Compromise: The Art of Navigating Win- ...*
  https://firstsachse.org/2023/08/effective-compromise-the-art-of-navigating-win-win-solutions/

- *How to Use Collaborative Problem-Solving Tools Effectively*
  https://www.linkedin.com/advice/1/how-can-you-ensure-effective-use-collaborative

- *Carol Dweck: A Summary of Growth and Fixed Mindsets*
  https://fs.blog/carol-dweck-mindset/

- *Overcoming Resistance To Change: 7 Strategies*
  https://primeast.com/us/insights/7-strategies-for-overcoming-resistance-to-change-in-the-workplace/

- *How to Master the Invisible Hand That Shapes Our Lives*
  https://jamesclear.com/feedback-loops

- *How To Learn from Your Mistakes and Achieve Better ...*
  https://www.indeed.com/career-advice/career-development/learn-from-the-mistakes

- *13 Emotional Intelligence Exercises, Activities & Worksheets*
  https://positivepsychology.com/emotional-intelligence-exercises/

- *The Role of Empathy in Communication*
  https://www.linkedin.com/pulse/role-empathy-communication-why-understanding-your-tyler-mehigh-mba

- *Understanding the Importance and Impact of Emotional ...*
  https://www.tajucoaching.com/blog/understanding-importance-and-impact-of-emotional-labor-in-workplace

- *Emotional Regulation: Skills, Exercises, & Strategies to ...*
  https://www.betterup.com/blog/emotional-regulation-skills

- *The dark side of social media in the workplace*
  https://www.sciencedirect.com/science/article/abs/pii/S0747563220001996

- *2023 Cyberbullying Data*
  https://cyberbullying.org/2023-cyberbullying-data

- *How AI Can Help You Develop Emotional Intelligence*
  https://www.forbes.com/councils/forbescoachescouncil/2023/03/24/how-ai-can-help-you-develop-emotional-intelligence/

- *Digital burnout: Managing mental health in remote work ...*
  https://www.counselling-directory.org.uk/articles/digital-burnout-managing-mental-health-in-remote-work-culture

- *Creating accountability networks for entrepreneurs*
  https://www.linkedin.com/pulse/creating-accountability-networks-entrepreneurs-mike-ducker

- *The Connection Between Vulnerability and Trust in Teams*
  https://emergenetics.com/blog/the-connection-between-vulnerability-

and-trust-in-teams/#:~:text=When%20you%20show%20vulnerability%2C%20it,allows%20for%20stronger%20team%20performance.

- *Leading with Compassion and Empathy in a Competitive ...*
  https://www.linkedin.com/pulse/leading-compassion-empathy-competitive-world-nurturing-matai-op0rf?trk=article-ssr-frontend-pulse_more-articles_related-content-card

- *How Office Design Impacts Employee Well-Being*
  https://www.canteen.com/research-and-trends/workplace-design-wellness/

- *How to create an action plan template (including examples)*
  https://monday.com/blog/project-management/action-plan-template/

- *The Power of Micro-Changes*
  https://www.kathysmith.com/the-power-of-micro-changes/

- *10 Best Goal Tracking Apps for 2025 (Free & Paid)*
  https://clickup.com/blog/goal-tracking-apps/

- *Using the Reflective Journal to Improve Practical Skills ...*
  https://pmc.ncbi.nlm.nih.gov/articles/PMC8394420/

- Josephson, Matthew. *Edison: A Biography*. Wiley, 1992.

- Rowling, J.K. "The Fringe Benefits of Failure, and the Importance of Imagination." Commencement Speech, Harvard University, 2008.

- Lazenby, Roland. *Michael Jordan: The Life*. Little, Brown and Company, 2014.

- Kelley, Kitty. *Oprah: A Biography*. Crown Archetype, 2010.

- Isaacson, Walter. *Einstein: His Life and Universe*. Simon & Schuster, 2007.

- Mayer, J. D., & Salovey, P. (1990). Emotional intelligence. *Imagination, Cognition and Personality*, 9(3), 185-211.

- Goleman, D. (1995). *Emotional intelligence: Why it can matter more than IQ*. New York: Bantam Books.

- Haselton, M. G., Nettle, D., & Andrews, P. W. (2005). The evolution of cognitive bias. In D. M. Buss (Ed.), *The Handbook of Evolutionary Psychology* (pp. 724-746). Wiley.

- Pronin, E., Lin, D. Y., & Ross, L. (2002). The bias blind spot: Perceptions of bias in self versus others. *Personality and Social Psychology Bulletin, 28*(3), 369-381.

- Baumeister, R. F., Campbell, J. D., Krueger, J. I., & Vohs, K. D. (2003). Does high self-esteem cause better performance, interpersonal success, happiness, or healthier lifestyles? *Psychological Science in the Public Interest, 4*(1), 1-44.

- Beck, J. S. (2011). *Cognitive behavior therapy: Basics and beyond* (2nd ed.). New York, NY: Guilford Press.

- Hofmann, S. G., Asnaani, A., Vonk, I. J. J., Sawyer, A. T., & Fang, A. (2012). The efficacy of cognitive behavioral therapy: A review of meta-analyses. *Cognitive Therapy and Research, 36*(5), 427-440.

- Heimberg, R. G., Becker, R. E., Goldfinger, K., & Vermilyea, J. A. (1987). Treatment of social phobia by exposure, cognitive restructuring, and homework assignments. *Journal of Nervous and Mental Disease, 175*(6), 355-364.

- Tortella-Feliu, M., Bornas, X., Llabrés, J., & Noguera, M. (2001). Computer-assisted exposure versus live graded exposure for fear of flying. *American Journal of Psychotherapy, 55*(4), 462-477.

- Doidge, N. (2007). *The brain that changes itself: Stories of personal triumph from the frontiers of brain science*. New York, NY: Viking.

- Prochaska, J. O., & DiClemente, C. C. (1983). Stages and processes of self-change of smoking: Toward an integrative model of change. *Journal of Consulting and Clinical Psychology, 51*(3), 390-395

- Locke, E. A., & Latham, G. P. (1990). *A theory of goal setting & task performance*. Englewood Cliffs, NJ: Prentice Hall.

- Festinger, L. (1957). *A theory of cognitive dissonance*. Stanford, CA: Stanford University Press.

- Evans, G. W., Li, D., & Whipple, S. S. (2013). Cumulative risk and child development. *Psychological Bulletin, 139*(6), 1342-1396.

- Kerr, M. E., & Bowen, M. (1988). *Family evaluation: An approach based on Bowen theory*. New York, NY: W. W. Norton & Company.

- Morrison, T., & Conaway, W. A. (2006). *Kiss, Bow, or Shake Hands: How to Do Business in Sixty Countries*. Avon, MA: Adams Media.

- Wurtz, E. (2005). A cross-cultural analysis of websites from high-context cultures and low-context cultures. *Journal of Computer-Mediated Communication, 11*(1), 13-38.

- Hall, E. T., & Hall, M. R. (1990). *Understanding cultural differences: Germans, French and Americans*. Yarmouth, ME: Intercultural Press.

- Ashkanasy, N. M., Zerbe, W. J., & Härtel, C. E. J. (Eds.). (2000). *Emotions in the workplace: Research, theory, and practice*. Westport, CT: Quorum Books.

- (2015). Wit & Wisdom. The Week, (1020), 19.

- Hooper, L. M. (2007). The application of attachment theory and family systems theory to the phenomena of parentification. *The Family Journal*, 15(3), 217-223. DOI: 10.1177/1066480707301290

OTHER BOOKS BY DELIA SIKES

EMPATHY UNLOCKED – LEARNING TO CONNECT IN A DISCONNECTED WORLD
PRACTICAL TECHNIQUES FOR ATTENTIVE COMMUNICATION, UNDERSTANDING PERSPECTIVES, SELF-COMPASSION, AND SETTING BOUNDARIES

https://www.amazon.com/dp/B0DKD28GQT

Other Books by Delia Sikes

Overthinking – The Silent Saboteur
Practical Techniques to Silence Your Inner Critic's Mind Chatter, Break Out of Analysis Paralysis, and End Self-Sabotage

https://www.amazon.com/dp/B0DNZF1MLL

Empathy and Overthinking
Navigating Your Inner and Interpersonal Worlds
Techniques for Attentive Communication, Understanding Perspectives, Quieting Mind Chatter, Setting Boundaries & Self-Compassion

https://www.amazon.com/dp/B0F3NYPL1T

French, Spanish and German versions of these books are coming soon.

Made in the USA
Las Vegas, NV
25 November 2025